MORMON ARTS

Presented by
The College of Fine Arts and Communications
Brigham Young University

The faculty of the departments of
Art, Communications, Music, and Speech and Dramatic Arts

With contributions from the departments of
English — College of Humanities
Dance — College of Physical Education
Environmental Design — College of Family Living
History — College of Social Sciences
and
Many participants beyond the Campus

MORMON ARTS

VOLUME ONE

Featuring articles and art work by
Mormon artists and authors

Lorin F. Wheelwright, Dean
General Editor
Lael J. Woodbury, Associate Dean
Associate Editor

Brigham Young University Press
Provo, Utah

The major significance of the symbol for the Mormon Festival of Arts relates to beliefs of The Church of Jesus Christ of Latter-day Saints.

Despite its mundane connotations, the square was chosen as the basic format because of its universally recognized strength and stability as a graphic element. Here, it also assumes the subtle profile of a book of holy writ. The stoic figure with his arm to the square symbolizes Mormon dedication of time and talent to a good cause. In contrast, the eternal round is suggested by curvilinear shapes representing the crucible or white fire of creativity. The five flamelike shapes have both aesthetic and spiritual meaning. The half figure, used primarily for emphasis, suggests that man may never achieve a wholeness of purpose or satisfaction in this life although he may devote his full energies in pursuit of those things which are "virtuous, lovely, or of good report or praiseworthy."

ALEX DARAIS

The opinions and statements expressed by contributors to *Mormon Arts, Volume I* are their own and do not necessarily reflect the views of The Church of Jesus Christ of Latter-day Saints or of Brigham Young University.

LCN: 72-93467
ISBN: 0-8425-0094-4
Brigham Young University Press, Provo, Utah
© by Brigham Young University Press. All rights reserved
Printed in the United States of America
1972 3.5M

PREFACE

The publication of this volume casts aside the edict that "nothing should ever be done for the first time." It began in the year of 1967 among an informal group of faculty and students who met on Sunday evenings to discuss art and Mormon belief. A leader of this movement was Dale Fletcher, an artist and teacher of sensitive spiritual convictions. He articulated clearly the idea that Mormon arts should be dedicated to the upbuilding of the kingdom of God on earth. Another spur to activity came from Elder Spencer W. Kimball of the Council of Twelve, who delivered the annual faculty lecture of that year on the theme of "Education for Eternity." In his charge to the University he said:

> The story of Mormonism has never yet been written nor painted nor sculptured nor spoken. It remains for inspired hearts and talented fingers yet to reveal themselves. They [artists] must be faithful, inspired, active Church members to give life and feeling and true perspective to a subject so worthy. . . . Our own talent, obsessed with dynamism from a CAUSE, could put into such a story life and heartbeats. . . .[1]

In this fertile ground, the incoming dean found opportunity to fulfill a lifetime dream of cultivating the arts as expressions of profound spiritual feelings: With the support of a talented student body, a competent faculty, and a responsive administration, the Mormon Festival of Arts blossomed. In 1969, the first festival presented two events: an art exhibit of paintings and sculpture by Mormon artists and the premier performance in America of *Pilgrim's Progress* by Ralph Vaughn Williams. In 1970 and 1971 the festival grew to include many events involving visiting artists, original compositions, literary works, and ballet. Other colleges on campus also participated. Attendance soared. The time seemed ripe to make some of the festival highlights more permanent. This book with its sound recording is the outcome.

Along with this outpouring of art forms on religious themes came a refinement of the original idea. Many symposia have treated the qualities of Mormon belief as they affect and inspire artists. A precise definition of Mormon Art still remains an open question. The works themselves best express their distinguishing characteristics. They demonstrate two basic concepts. One stresses the importance of finding and possessing truth and beauty wherever they exist. This opens the whole world of artistic endeavor to Mormon enjoyment. The other stresses unique Mormon values and ways of expressing them in aesthetic forms.

This volume offers some premises and principles that seem germane to both viewpoints. A rationale for the book appears in a series of articles beginning with "Is There a Mormon Art?" Both visual and auditory examples of current Mormon works of art are presented. These exemplify Mormon art in terms of style, medium, and personality.

The reader is cautioned not to draw final conclusions from this volume. It does not presume to delimit Mormon art. The subtitle, *Volume I,* embodies the spirit of the work. Other volumes must follow until a comprehensive body of art works, literature, and aesthetics infuse our Mormon culture. Also, this work has purposely limited its chief interest to the more unique expression of Mormon values. All that is "praiseworthy and of good report" cannot be included because of limitations in space. This does not imply a narrowness of interest. Most of the artistic endeavors of the College of Fine Arts and Communications at Brigham Young University would fall into a broad category.

The unique contribution of this work, if there is one, is its dedication to the sincere expressions of Mormon artists who find inspiration in their religion to create. Those who appear here do so because they believe that a work of art which stirs the human heart to love God and fellowman should have superior form, substance, and expression. In this volume we present printed and recorded examples of many such works. Although visiting artists have added color and interest to this endeavor, the majority of the work has come from the faculty and student body of Brigham Young University.

Reports from viewers, listeners, and contributors to the festivals have been systematically collected and analyzed. Their enthusiastic response encourages this publication. Although it may serve more as an hors d'oeuvre than a full meal, it justifies its existence if it stirs the appetite of the reader for continued experience with and enjoyment of Mormon arts.

LORIN F. WHEELWRIGHT

---

[1] Elder Spencer W. Kimball, "Education for Eternity," preschool address to faculty and staff presented at Brigham Young University, Provo, Utah, September 12, 1967.

Harris Fine Arts Center, Brigham Young University — home, Mormon Festival of Arts

ACKNOWLEDGMENTS

This book is a cooperative venture by artists, musicians, composers, writers, University administrators, and a host of students whose efforts in the first three festivals of Mormon arts are reflected here. Whenever a work has been used, the name of the contributor is given. To each, a special *thank you* is due for creating his work and granting permission for its use. In addition, special recognition is due the following:

Richard Bird, for his design of the book and preparation of all layouts and paste-ups preparatory to publication.

Allen Cornwall, for promotion of the third festival and his persistence in editorial research.

Heber G. Wolsey and Edwin J. Butterworth of University Relations, for press releases and publicity of festival events.

Helen D. Pomeroy, secretary and chief typist of manuscripts.

The Brigham Young University Press, for technical editing and typesetting.

The Electronic Media Department, for making the recordings and John Neal, for mixing and preparing master tapes.

Allied Record Company, for pressing phonograph records.

Wetzel O. Whitaker, director of the Motion Picture Studio, for use of *Man's Search for Happiness*.

Wheelwright Lithographing Company, for color separations and press work.

The magazine, *Art in America*, for color separations of C.C.A. Christensen's Mormon Panorama.

Mountain States Bindery, for cover and binding.

The department chairmen and committee members of the College of Fine Arts and Communications who designed and administered each Mormon Festival of Arts, with particular recognition of:

Lael J. Woodbury, associate dean of the college and chairman of events.

Floyd E. Breinholt and Douglas A. Stout, chairmen of the Department of Art, with Dale H. Fletcher, Ronald D. Deane, and Gary Smith in charge of exhibitions. Alex Darais, designer of the Festival symbol.

J. Morris Richards and Edwin O. Haroldsen, chairmen of the Department of Communications, and Wallace M. Barrus, director of photography.

A. Harold Goodman, chairman of the Department of Music, and Harrison Powley as expediter of events.

Parley W. Newman, chairman of the Department of Speech and Dramatic Arts, and Charles Henson and Charles Whitman.

Milo Baughman and associates for direction on environmental needs.

Dallin H. Oaks, President, Brigham Young University; Ernest L. Wilkinson, President during the Mormon arts festivals of 1969, 1970, and 1971; Ben E. Lewis, Executive Vice-President; Robert K. Thomas, Academic Vice-President; and Robert J. Smith, Associate Vice-President — all of whom have supported the festival and this publication with administrative decisions and financial appropriations.

The college deans who have lent assistance through their faculties:

Bruce B. Clark, Dean, College of Humanities
Milton F. Hartvigsen, Dean, College of Physical Education
Martin B. Hickman, Dean, College of Social Sciences
Blaine R. Porter, Dean, College of Family Living

A panel of distinguished scholars who have read the manuscript and offered editorial suggestions and encouragement for its publication: Henry Eyring, Dean Emeritus of the Graduate School, University of Utah; Keith Engar, Head of the Department of Drama, University of Utah; Chauncey Riddle, Dean of the Graduate School, BYU; and Professors Reed H. Bradford, Truman G. Madsen, and Edwin O. Haroldsen, of the Brigham Young University Faculty.

The Board of Trustees, Brigham Young University, for providing the superb facilities of the Harris Fine Arts Center and for supporting the arts in Mormon culture; and Elder Spencer W. Kimball, whose address "Education for Eternity," has inspired this creative effort.

vi

CONTENTS

REPRODUCTIONS OF ART AND PHOTOGRAPHY

IS THERE A MORMON ART?

When artists are asked to submit paintings, musical compositions, photographs, and other art objects to a Mormon Festival of Arts, they ask, "What is 'Mormon' about art?" The question is fundamental. The answer does not appear clearly at once. But, as this festival grows and as its participants search their culture and their own souls for answers, distinctions do emerge. This book serves to encourage the sharing of ideas and concepts of many artists and thinkers on the subject.

It is ambitiously entitled *Mormon Arts, Volume I*, implying other volumes will follow. This is our way of saying that we are on a threshold of artistic development within the Mormon culture and that this festival is expanding our awareness of the spiritual power of our religion to inspire artistic endeavor. From such awareness, hopefully, will emerge artistic expressions as characteristic of the Mormon people and as "peculiar" to this world as are our theology and resultant patterns of personal and family life.

One might ask, in answer to the basic question posed here, "Is there a Greek art, a Roman art, a Chinese art, or an American Indian art?" Space does not permit a treatise on the characteristics of style that distinguish schools or periods of art. We assume that there are such and that they reflect the basic ethos of their originators. We can assume that men paint, sculpt, design, build buildings, and make music that express their basic beliefs. In many historical instances, the arts are the only remaining clues to such beliefs for us to study. This volume assumes that the arts do reveal significant characteristics of the people who create them.

If a future archaeological expedition were to discover the residue of a Mormon Festival of Arts, what could it deduce, from the evidence, regarding the people who created the works? In that answer lies what is "Mormon" about this festival. Such an answer points the way toward future development of the festival as an honest and comprehensive expression of Mormon culture.

At the moment, Mormon art reflects an image that is somewhat blurred because its distinctive characteristics are diffused rather than focused in a unique style. As the examples herein illustrate, different artists find a wide diversity of expressive means. This is to be expected as the process of discovery and expression progresses. Church artists are now researching their spiritual experiences and expressive skills to communi-

EV THORPE, *Artist*

THE SEAGULLS — One of the cherished stories of Mormon history and the settlement of the Great Salt Lake Valley is the saving of the crops by the seagulls. After the first company of pioneers — under the leadership of Brigham Young — made the trek west, it was imperative that crops be planted and harvested to feed the great migration that was to follow. To the utter dismay of the early settlers, just as a bumper crop began to sprout, a horde of black crickets came as if from nowhere and began devouring the budding plants. A fear arose that the crops would be lost and the people would starve to death in the new wilderness settlement. They fought desperately against the hordes of insects but to no avail. Then they turned to prayer, and miraculously there appeared a white cloud of seagulls. At first, the settlers feared that the birds had come to join the crickets in destroying the new crop, but to their great relief, the seagulls began to eat the crickets.

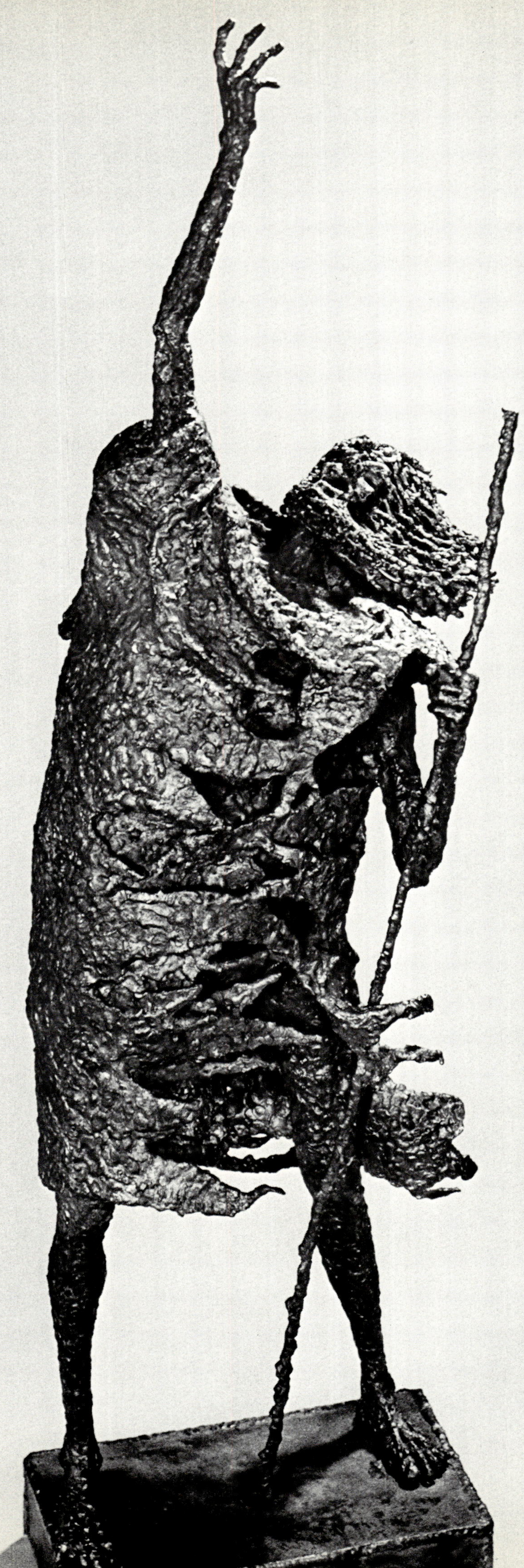

cate their convictions in aesthetic forms. Time is an ally in this development as is the stimulating exposure of Mormon art at Brigham Young University. A new generation of artists and composers is now seeing and hearing original Mormon works which arouse in them new insights and imaginative forms by which to embody their own beliefs — many of which lie dormant for want of expression.

At this point we might look for clues. Already, we can see certain distinguishing lines that infuse Mormon artistic expression.

1. *Men are that they might have joy.* This absolute in Mormon belief dispels pessimism. Although Mormons know that the way to perfection is difficult and that disappointments are inevitable as they face conflicts enroute, they also know that faith creates hope, and that hope is an opposite of despair. A spirit of buoyancy infuses Mormon expectations and finds expression in Mormon art. Emphasis on misery, degradation and hopelessness are consistently absent. Faith in the healing power of Christ replaces these negative values.

2. *Man is an eternal being, created in the image of God.* This high value of man, which makes his soul sacred and priceless among all of creation, distinguishes the Mormon viewpoint from contemporary materialism. To Mormons, life is not cheap; it is a prized possession, something to protect, nurture, develop, and love. Artistically, such belief finds expression in reverence for human life. Children are loved, old people are respected and cared for, all human beings are considered brothers with a common, divine parentage. This belief negates the pleasure some contemporary artists take in expressing the cruelty of man to man, a sadistic pleasure in suffering, and the cesspool view of man's excesses. Mormon artists work to express the divine in man by revealing his beauty of spirit, by revering the human body, by considering the act of procreation as sacred, and by avoiding the contemporary vogue of exploiting hedonistic sex. They recognize human depravity and cruelty as manifestations of the "natural man." In seeking to reveal the spiritual man, they hope to express his divinity rather than his devilishness, and in so doing they reinforce their pursuit

---

THE PROPHET — On various occasions, I have created illustrations for the Sunday School and other divisions of the Church. This work, involving considerable research on the Church and its members, has given me a profound appreciation for the trials encountered by this group. I have been so impressed by the indomitable, resurgent character of these people that I wanted to capture it in some way. THE PROPHET is an attempt to display this irrepressible spirit and to express in some measure the invincible faith of those who suffer adversity while refusing to capitulate to injustice or other forms of evil.

ROBERT V. BULLOUGH, *Artist*

POTATO BARN, by Merrill L. Gogan, upper left
A HILL TO CLIMB, by Alex B. Darais, upper right
LAMANITE FOSTER BROTHER,
by Roland L. Lee, lower left

We believe in being honest, true, chaste, benevolent, virtuous, and in doing good to all men; indeed, we may say that we follow the admonition of Paul — We believe all things, we hope all things, we have endured many things, and hope to be able to endure all things. If there is anything virtuous, lovely, or of good report or praiseworthy, we seek after these things.

Joseph Smith,
13 Article of Faith

of eternal perfection and their goal of becoming Christlike in control of human emotions.

3. *It must needs be, that there is an opposition in all things.* A basic tenet of Mormon faith holds that free agency in human thought and action is essential to man's moral development. Hence, man must apply his value system to his real world of optional behavior.

Temptation, in the sense of *trial* rather than *enticement to evil,* thus becomes a requirement for spiritual growth. The aesthetic necessity of showing opposing forces, particularly in drama, is balanced in Mormon art by the value of showing how evil is overcome by forces of righteousness. Tragedy as an art form does not imply defeat. Mormons feel deeply the tragic events of Joseph Smith's martyrdom. They empathize with the sufferings of the pioneers. But, their drama and literature rarely employ tragedy in its classic form. This may be due to lack of creative effort, or it may reflect the desire of Mormon authors and artists to express the triumph of the human spirit in other forms. (See page 58 for a notable exception.)

4. *All truth and all good are of God.* This comprehensiveness of a divine gospel leads Mormons to search the whole world and all intellectual fields for enlightment. Hence, great emphasis is given to education — not merely to formal schooling during formative years — but to education in its eternal continuum, neatly conceptualized as "eternal

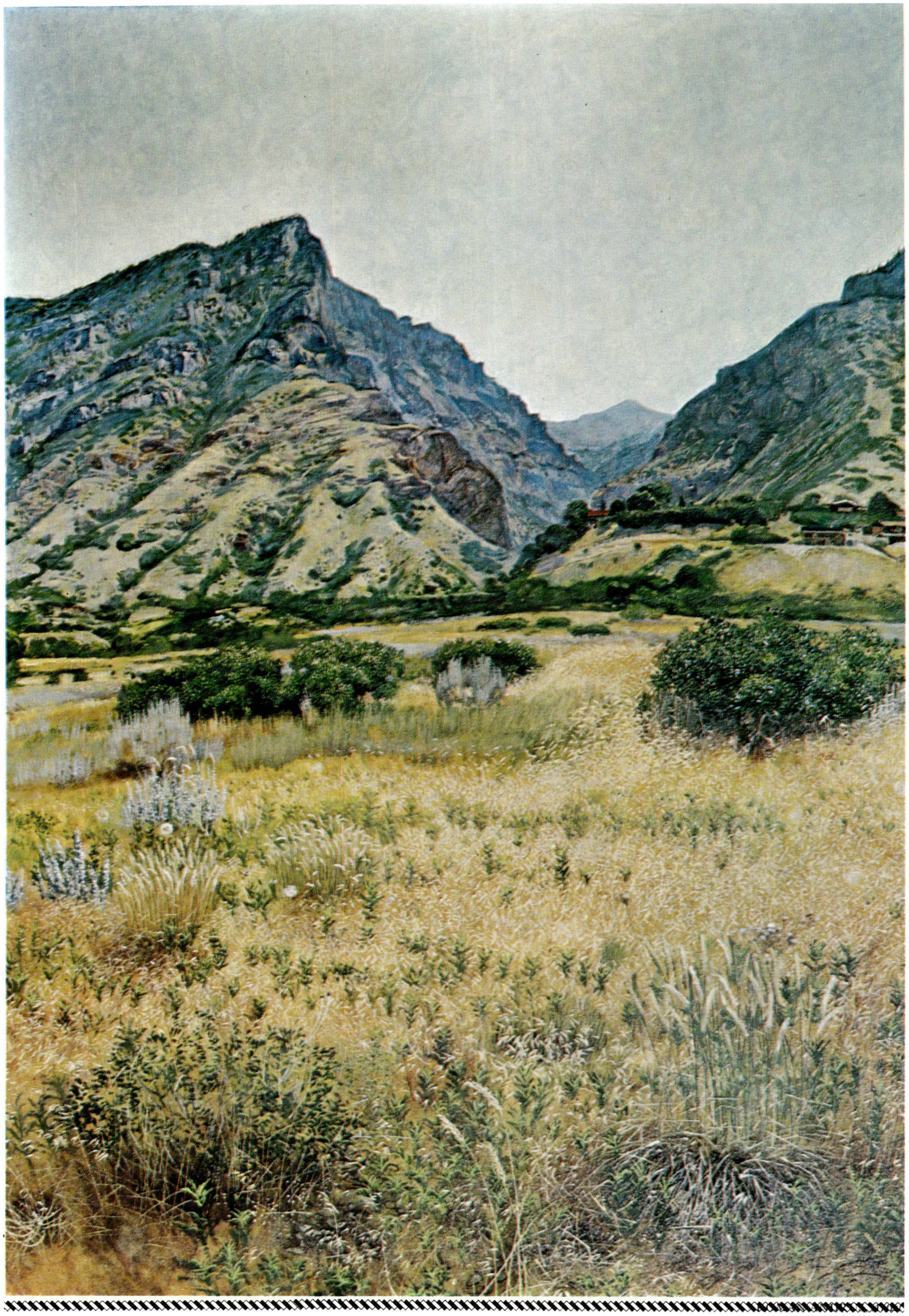

progression.'' The approaching millennium is seen as a thousand years of perfecting the self. The Celestial Kingdom is seen as a place to develop one's spiritual and creative powers until the fullness of Godhood is achieved. Mortality is a compressed period where every moment counts and where certain physical experiences can be gained as in no other sphere of development. Time, consequently, becomes critical — never to be wasted, always to be invested in worthwhile learning. Opportunity is everywhere, even amid agonizing crises. From such a viewpoint, the dedicated Mormon seeks

ABINADI — THE PROPHET — For Abinadi, integrity was more important than life. The flames which flared around him and brought death illumined a spirit which chose to declare the truth rather than to be popular with the King and the crowds. This painting was conceived as a tribute to those who raise unwilling mankind to recognize truth that popular voices often cry out against.
"But this much I tell you, what you do with me, after this, shall be as a type and a shadow of things which are to come." Mosiah 13:10.   ROMAN ANDRUS, *Artist*

the truth — extracted by the sweat of his brow — as revealed in Scripture, as told by living prophets, and as sealed in the handiwork of God. Study is a way of life to a devoted Mormon, and such study encompasses all spiritual and physical evidences, all cultures and all truth as understood by men of perception. In the artistic expression of such pursuit, one sees an honest attempt to find truth and beauty in all of God's creations.

In this volume, a section appears on principles that synthesize the fields of religion, science, and aesthetics. Illustrations hint at the comprehensive scope of these principles. It is characteristically "Mormon" to articulate such principles and to invite others to share their meaning. In contrast, much of contemporary art and critical comment exploits the confusion of men who are torn between disbelief in traditional religious values and vain hope in secular philosophies. A breadth of interest and a search for beauty and truth are admirable traits of Latter-day Saints in the world of today. Where a member is artistically inclined, these qualities distinguish his aesthetic expression.

5. *The gospel of Jesus Christ has been restored in its fullness and is the only way to personal and world peace.* This conviction leads the devout Mormon to pattern his life after that of the Master and to build the Master's kingdom here on the earth. Because of his dedication, the Mormon artist would hope to lead others to this insight by his artistic expressions. This might be considered by non-Mormons as a subordination of artistic values to didactic values. The section of this book treating "instrumental" versus "consummatory" values of art identifies some spiritual aspirations that Mormons hold in the highest of consummatory value. When these values are expressed aesthetically, a Mormon artist does precisely for his culture what the ancient Greek artist did for his, or the Chinese, or the American Indian or others have done for theirs. It is in this realm of concern that the artist can hope to make his work expressive of his belief and identifiable to any investigator of Mormon culture.

DIXIE STONE — For me, this painting records a religious experience. When I sit in nature and become a student of the only true Creator, I am humbled and brought to feel my nothingness as compared to the monumentality of God's creation. My visual experience, though finite, may reveal energy, vitality, principles of color contrasts, organization, design, order, and love to the viewer. This painting is not immediately recognizable as Mormon art, just as the real world, bearing its Maker's signature, is often overlooked and the great lessons to be learned from it and the beautiful spirit to be found in it are seldom recognized.

Dixie Stone is a testimony of God's creative powers, of his love for us in providing our environment. My vocabulary in bearing this witness may be elementary, but that fact only reveals the promise of an eternity.

DAVID LEE RINDLISBACHER, *Artist*

For Zion must increase in beauty, and in holiness . . .

D & C 82:14

DAVID L. RINDLISBACHER

This volume is divided into two main sections. The first half presents, in text, a series of six articles on the aesthetics of Mormon art. The second half deals with special projects of the Mormon arts festivals that illumine the current scene of Mormon artistic culture. Throughout this volume are many statements that express feelings regarding the historical and contemporary religious experience of the Latter-day Saints. Some of these feelings are expressed in music that can better be heard than seen. For this purpose a recording is included in the volume. .

Art style, as evidenced in abstraction versus representationalism, has not been proscribed either by the festival nor by the University. Such matters are left to the taste of contributors, juries, and participants. The editors of this volume challenge the viewer to seek truth in all things, including the sincere expressions of artists whose styles differ from his own comfortable preferences. A predominant viewpoint of the editors is that questions of purpose in art overshadow style in importance. Since this is the first volume, it seems appropriate to deal with broad principles. For this reason the book is more a view from the threshold than a comprehensive summation.

Our introduction "Is There a Mormon Art?" is followed by "Art as a Joy of Man and Instrument of God." This second section attempts to illuminate two basic functions of art, namely, the instrumental and consummatory. In the first 140 years of Church history, much emphasis has been given to instrumental values of art. It is our opinion that we are now approaching an increasing emphasis upon consummatory values. The focus of these two approaches is sharpened by a brief review of the aesthetic philosophy of John Dewey and Leo Tolstoy. Their views are representative of some Mormon artists and are included to guide the reader to a clearer understanding of art criticism as applied to Mormon values. Statements by Mormon artists in this volume complement this clarification, as related to specific works.

The article "Seeking Aesthetic Experience" is designed to lead the reader into the fascinating development of greater insight and enjoyment of the arts. Five steps are described that characterize all learning experiences. These are designed to help the reader find himself so he might move from whatever plateau he may now occupy to a point above and beyond his present interest.

The section entitled "Divine Creation" projects a basic belief of Mormonism; namely, God is the Supreme Creator. His creations are the models for man's artistic attempts. The aesthetic quality of the earth and its philosophical importance to Latter-day Saints are explored to orient the reader for the next section, "Man Creates in

the Image of God." Here are presented specific principles that unite divine revelation, physical discovery, and aesthetic expression. Several examples illustrate how these principles support a unified view. This exploration challenges Mormon artists, scientists, and theologians to develop a unified theory of man's relationship to man, to his environment, and to his eternal destiny.

The concluding section of the first half of the book develops the idea that "Art Expresses Opposition in All Things." Here, again, we postulate a theological base for an aesthetic reality and attempt to relate the spiritual principle of opposing forces to the basic tools of the creative artist.

Throughout these pages are reproductions of paintings and sculpture that exemplify the aesthetic and religious principles under discussion. They are drawn from the exhibitions of the first three Mormon arts festivals.

The second half of the book deals with specific areas of artistic concern, such as the works of C. C. A. Christensen, an early Mormon painter; the poetic, dramatic, musical, and photographic creations of contemporary Latter-day Saints; and the challenge of sustaining an

FALL: BLUE POINT and NAUVOO REFLECTIONS — **These pieces are from a group of paintings that I have entitled the Nauvoo Series. I have endeavored to present my impressions of the country landscape that so enamored the early Mormon settlers. The rich and varied landscape of Iowa and Illinois offered many formal challenges that intrigued me as an artist. Although much has been written describing the early Saints' love for the land, little attempt has been made to present the visual properties and visual poetry of this portion of the Midwest. Mormon heritage is found in this land, and I have attempted to express its meaning through many studies of a peculiar people and their environment.**

BART J. MORSE, *Artist*

environment that nurtures the buoyant spirit. The volume closes with a listing of people and events contributing to the Festival and a prayer of gratitude and aspiration.

Again, Is There a Mormon Art? Yes, if one can see an emerging flower in the growing seed. It is characterized by a spirit of optimism, faith in the eternal destiny of man, expression of opposing forces without defeat, reverence for God's creativity in nature, and revealed truth as the basis of peace. Styles of artistic expression are crossing a threshold toward maturity and are best seen in specific works. This volume presents many such works and breaks ground for much development yet to come.

LORIN F. WHEELWRIGHT

BART J. MORSE, *Artist*

ART AS JOY OF MAN AND INSTRUMENT OF GOD

DAY OF THE LAMANITE — I created this painting because of my extreme interest in the Indian Placement Program of the Church. The boy kneeling on the left is my foster son, Jerry Plummer, a Navajo from Gallup, New Mexico. In the four years he has been part of our family, we have been amazed at the progress he has made as a priesthood holder and as a potential leader of his people. The boy in the middle, Verdi Stone from Arizona, was chosen for the painting because of his classic features and fine spiritual attitude. The boy on the right, David Bona, is a friend from my ward.

I have a love and respect for the Indian people. I was raised in eastern Utah near the Ute reservation and spent the summer of 1964 living and working with the youth in a recreation camp for the Ute tribe.

One of my most enjoyable duties was to load some of these young people into a bus and drive to MIA on Tuesday evenings. It was most inspiring to watch them stand and recite the MIA theme, which that year was the promise given to the Lamanites by Moroni in the Book of Mormon. (Moroni 10:4.)

In general, the Indian people have a simple spiritual outlook on life and are teachable and humble. It is obvious that they are beginning to realize the great promises that the Lord has given them. This is the reason I chose the title, Day of the Lamanite, for my painting.

A. VALOY EATON, *Artist*

1970 Mormon Festival of Arts Purchase Award Winner

Insight regarding the nature and function of Mormon art can be gained by examining two basic concepts relating to the purpose of art. These concepts are "consummatory" and "instrumental." They represent two different value systems.

A consummatory value is one derived from an activity that is worth pursuing for its own sake. It relates to the appreciation and enjoyment of art. An instrumental value is one derived from an activity pursued as means to an end. It relates, for example, to art created to sell a product, a personality, or an idea. Instrumental values include the skills, techniques, and social understandings used to pursue consummatory values.

Among the ultimate consummatory values for which men strive is the value of "happiness," or "joy." If we examine "health," our consummatory values might be: I want to feel good, rested, at ease, alive, clean, unpolluted, well coordinated; and sensitive in taste, hearing, and seeing. I want to "run and not be weary and walk and not faint." I want to enjoy flavors and textures, sounds, shapes, colors, and all those things that satisfy my emotional hunger. I want to feel temperatures that are comfortable and use furniture, chairs, tables, beds, and the like, that fit me. In a word, this kind of creative comfort and fitness is happiness. When we think of health in its instrumental set of values, we think of sleeping, exercising, eating, drinking, breathing, working, playing, golfing, fishing, and dozens of other pursuits that lead to the consummatory values.

If we examine fishing as an activity, the consummatory value is the pleasure we get from it. The instrumental value is the fish we cook and eat. A sportsman will often give away his fish. He has had his pay in the fun of catching it. One definition of work and play is based on whether an activity produces enjoyment or boredom. If it is fun, it is high in consummatory value. If it is irksome, it is low in such value, and workers demand more pay. Labor strife stems from loss of personal pride in the guild where joy of accomplishment and beauty of craftsmanship were once major compensations. Now, men often feel forsaken in production

lines. Hence they organize into unions to guarantee themselves financial compensation in proportion to lack of consummatory compensation. Enlightened management attempts to provide more consummatory value through pleasant surroundings and pride in team achievement.

Another example of conflict of values involves a former president and his portrait. A dispute arose between Lyndon Johnson and the painter of his portrait, Peter Hurd. Mr. Hurd painted in a style to express himself and to give himself satisfaction. Mr. Johnson, as the subject, was instrumental in this process. Therefore, if Mr. Hurd felt that he should make changes of line, shape, or color to effect a more pleasing and aesthetically satisfying composition to meet his own inner hunger, Mr. Johnson could become very much a secondary consideration in the process. Mr. Johnson objected to this.

Mr. Hurd has a prototype in Rembrandt, who was once asked to paint the important citizens of his town. He did so in *The Night Watch*. He disregarded their personal desires, however, and created a composition to fit his own aesthetic taste. Opposition arose against Mr. Rembrandt; he became an outcast. His words were

THE MARTYRDOM — These paintings are of both a physical and spiritual importance. They are physical in the sense that an act of murder is taking place and spiritual in that a prophet is sealing his testimony with his blood. I was more interested in creating a feeling than in conveying the situation. The paintings are realistic in terms of historical fact and spiritual manifestation, rather than photographic realism. My intent in these paintings was to have the viewer receive the spiritual influence I felt while being involved with this important period of the Church.

GARY E. SMITH, *Artist*

GARY E. SMITH, *Artist*

FORCES OF EVIL, upper left
AN ACT OF DEFENSE, left
DEATH OF THE PROPHET, right
THE MARTYRED, next page,
1971 Mormon Festival of Arts
Purchase Award Winner

. . . it must needs be, that there is opposition in all things.

2 NEPHI 2:11

EDWARD E. HUMPHREYS, Artist

undoubtedly quite similar to those of Mr. Hurd, and the text of the citizens' response probably paralleled that of Mr. Johnson. The issue is really, whose happiness is to be served? An old adage generally prevails: He who pays the fiddler calls the tune. But there is always the other dimension of criticism, namely, the unseen, untapped audience of the future. What will those critics say? The generations since the time of Rembrandt have voted for Rembrandt and against the burghers of Holland. Only the future can tell us whether Mr. Johnson or Mr. Hurd has come closest to creating the greatest happiness for the greatest number.

Art and the Church

Having examined instrumental and consummatory values in general, let us direct our attention to art as used in The Church of Jesus Christ of Latter-day Saints. What are the values involved in this context? The Church teaches as a fundamental doctrine that "men are, that they might have joy."[1]

This says, in essence, that joy is a religious experience that transcends immediate and transitory delights. It projects man's desire for well-being into an eternal dimension.

Following are some consummatory values of Mormonism. These are the kinds of spiritual joy toward which faithful Latter-day Saints strive.

- To feel inner peace from certainty regarding one's place in the universe.
- To feel spiritual renewal through sacred ordinances.
- To feel triumphant in victory of good over evil.
- To feel an ecstasy in one's personal progress toward perfection and empathy for the progress of others.
- To feel expanded in spirit through the brotherhood of all men.
- To feel such closeness to God as to *be* god-like.

The Church aims to enhance such values in all men. It uses art instrumentally to induce conversion. For those who become members, the Church uses art instrumentally to remind them of the consummatory values yet to be realized in eternity. The Church also uses art, to a limited degree, to induce aesthetic joy here and now. Resolving these multiple uses of art to the satisfaction of nonmembers and members alike presents a most complex and difficult administrative process.

TO MAKE A WHOLE — "All parts of creation are related: all parts belong to a whole. Basic units of design employ twos and threes or their combinations." (See page 36.)

The art on Temple Square in Salt Lake City, Utah, illustrates this kind of decision making. When Brigham Young decided to build a tabernacle organ, he told Joseph Ridges, "Joseph, if you will make that organ, there is nothing you want which you cannot have." He then allowed an expenditure of $900 — everything that could be spared from the Church funds — for Joseph Ridges to go to Boston and New York to purchase parts. The rest of that original organ, consisting of 2,000 pipes, was made in the Salt Lake Valley. President Young was a frequent visitor to the workshop and on one occasion said, "We can't preach the gospel unless we have good music. I am waiting patiently for the organ to be finished, and then we can sing the gospel into the hearts of the people."[2]

TESTIMONY MEETING — The old gentleman in the picture lives in my ward and agreed to pose in the chapel in a characteristic posture. He insisted on prayer at each sitting.

I have tried to convey the quiet dignity of a testimony meeting and man's reaction to testimony at different ages from toddler to teen-ager to young father. In this sense it becomes a modern revival of the Middle Ages' "Ages of Man" theme.

L. ROSS JOHNSON, *Artist*

Think:
Worlds from now
What might we be? --
We,
Who are seed
Of Deity.

Trevor Southey, *Artist*
Carol Lynn Pearson,
Beginnings, Provo, Utah: Trilogy Arts, 1969

This clear statement of the instrumental use of musical art on Temple Square has guided basic policy ever since. Music is used not only to sing the gospel into the hearts of the Saints but into the hearts of every visitor who will come and listen, or who will tune in and listen. It is the practice of the choir and the organists when they perform concerts, either on Temple Square or on tour, to include on the program a favorite Mormon hymn. Whenever possible, the text of that hymn is printed. Thus, the music and poetry become vehicles by which a preachment is made. As the choir has performed in concerts over the land, music critics are attracted both by instrumental *and* consummatory values. Critics comment on the choir's "crisp, clear attacks," "admirable phrasing," "musicianly interpretation." *Time* magazine has observed that the choir's two Berlin concerts in 1956 produced more than musical pleasure.

Everywhere they are stirring up waves of good feelings and applause. Salt Lake City's Mormon Tabernacle Choir is a smash hit in Europe.[3]

Berlin's *Telegraf* said: "This was not only music, but the building of a human bridge."[4]

The unprecedented goodwill built by the choir on its radio and television broadcasts and by the organ over many years of successful noonday concerts paved the way for decisions by Church authorities to use visual arts to induce conversion. Missionary presentations using a sequence of illustrations were a notable success at the New York World's Fair in 1966. Following the fair, these same illustrations, plus others, were moved to the Information Bureau on Temple Square.

At a cottage meeting of artists who were lamenting the fact that these pictures are "not very good art," a member spoke up as follows:

I am not an artist and I have belonged to your church for only nine months, so I hesitate to speak in such a learned group. You say the paintings on Temple Square are not very good art. Perhaps they are not, but they are very efficient as teachers. I am here tonight because I happened to stay over several hours between planes and took a run into Temple Square when your very efficient guides escorted me through the Information Bureau. As they told me the story of the Church, they pointed out the various paintings and other exhibits

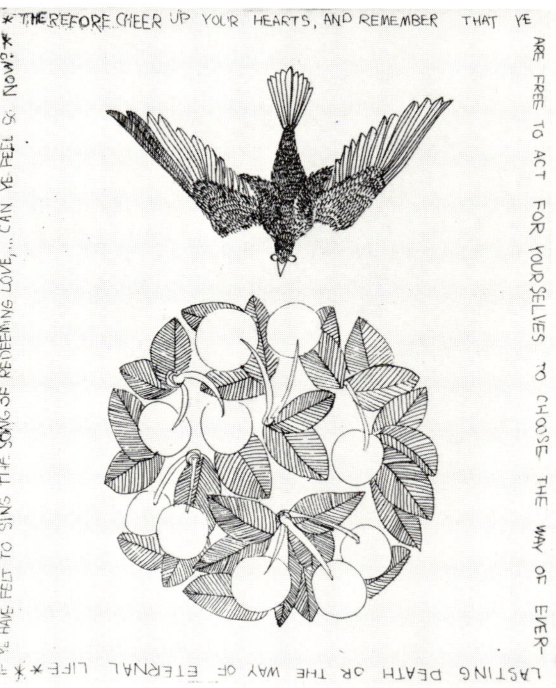

DESCENT FROM THE CROSS — **The pathos of Christ's sacrifice is portrayed in this painting. A personal realization of the transgressional agony that you and I have caused the Saviour is the motivation for the mood of the composition. Opposite**   FRANZ M. JOHANSEN, *Artist*

PROMISE — **This symbolizes the principle of resurrection through the use of the cocoon image — as the butterfly will emerge from its deathlike sleep, so will man come forth (awake) from his death state in the glory of the resurrection. I am very interested in communicating my feelings about the gospel on several levels. I am searching for new symbols that will say something, that will indicate my philosophy of the eternal principles of truth without descending to the level of simple story telling or illustration. Right**   JAMES C. CHRISTENSEN, *Artist*

WHAT IS COURAGE, William Whitaker, Artist, top

BETWEEN — **This is a symbolic illustration of two scriptures from the Book of Mormon (2 Nephi 10:23 and Alma 5:26) with script of verses. The source for the symbolic idea was a book of medieval Christian symbolism, in which the cherry symbolizes evil and darkness. The two scriptures indicate the opportunity we have to choose between good and evil.**

MARILYN R. MILLER, *Artist*

15

which illustrated that story. In one hour's time I realized that I had found a religious background and doctrine which moved and stirred me. When I returned to the East, I made further inquiry and study and joined the Church soon thereafter. What those pictures may lack in artistic quality, they make up in efficiency.

At that point, those who had been most critical of aesthetic values acknowledged that art serves more than one function. In "A Study of Representative Examples of Art Works Fostered by the Mormon Church, with an Analysis of the Aesthetic Value of These Works," Monte B. DeGraw analyzes several theories of aesthetics and makes a survey of nineteen separate works of art sponsored by the Church. These works include such pieces as the Handcart Pioneer Monument, Winter Quarters Monument, This Is the Place Monument, Seagull Monument, stained glass windows in the Salt Lake Temple,

MORONI — This suspended sculpture in bronze presents Moroni as the bold, yet sensitive person that I feel him to be from the Book of Mormon and the witness of the Prophet Joseph Smith. Hopefully, this visual statement expresses a gospel truth to the viewer to the same extent that it does to the artistic creator. Even as there was only one Moroni, there is only one bronze of this figure, since the wax mold had to be melted to provide a matrix for the casting.

CHASE SHEPARD, *Artist*　　LORIN F. WHEELWRIGHT, *Photographer*

Hyrum Smith Monument, and Book of Mormon paintings. His thesis states:

The major emphasis of the art works examined in this study was didactic and commemorative in purpose and theme. Aesthetic embellishment and artistic enrichment of church buildings and grounds were intended purposes of the art under consideration. However, in but few of the art works do the aesthetic qualities emerge with conviction to overpower the literary, story telling and imitative connotations. A work in which the aesthetic values were expressed more successfully is the "Angel Moroni Statue" on the Los Angeles Temple. In this work the emphasis is more nearly on originality and form rather than on didactic, imitative elements.

His conclusion states:

Themes are concerned primarily with the practices and institutions connected with the Mormon people. None of the art works studied are influenced by themes connected with the outside world. Aesthetic purpose has not been ignored in some examples. But this purpose is minimized because of strong didactic emphasis. [5]

MARGARET GREEVER, *Artist*

The Artistic Goals of Brigham Young University

A hunger for aesthetic experience is evident among members of the Church. Particularly is there a restlessness among young artists. Many consider the illustrative and storytelling aspects of art as too restrictive. They yearn to inject more consummatory values into the art form itself.

Some of these young artists are creating in idioms that appear strange to the past generation. There are some critics who condemn this strangeness as want of sincerity. Almost every notable artist of the past whose work has set a new mode of expression has fallen under such criticism by his contemporaries.

The fine arts programs of Brigham Young University reflect many historical influences. Foremost among these is the emphasis upon form by John Dewey and the priority of religious content held by Leo Tolstoy.

In his essay "What Is Art?" Tolstoy places as most important among the criteria of greatness in art *individuality*, *clearness*, and *sincerity*. He states that these "decide the merit of a work of art as art apart from the subject matter." He affirms that "art, like speech, is a means of communication, and therefore of progress, that is, of the movement of humanity forward towards perfection." [6]

John Dewey in *Art as Experience* states:

Whatever narrows the boundaries of the material fit to be used in art hems in also the artistic sincerity of the individual artist. It does not give fair play as outlet to his vital interest. It forces his perception into channels previously worn into ruts and clips the wings of his imagination. [7]

Both Dewey and Tolstoy agree that *sincerity* is the essential quality of valid aesthetic expres-

CRUCIFIX — In the past, artists have chosen to depict the crucifixion as a somber, sorrowful occasion. To paint another crucifixion in greys — in pale browns, would be for me useless repetition. I chose instead lively strong colors and even took away the cross. In this way He almost seems to be a life force growing up across the format, not a carcass draped over wooden beams. The angle of view focuses on the crowd's reaction rather than on the face of Christ.

---

sion. But Tolstoy takes the unique position that one can distinguish what is good and bad in art by reference to content. Of good art he says that "the religious perception of our time in its widest and most practical application is the consciousness that our well being, both material and spiritual, individual and collective, temporal and eternal, lies in the growth of brotherhood among men in their loving harmony with one another." [8]

Tolstoy is more explicit in clarifying how Christianity has changed the basic content of art — or, rather, how it should have changed it

WILLIAM WHITAKER, Artist

SAMUEL SMITH, FIRST MORMON MISSIONARY — Carrying his case filled with the first edition of the Book of Mormon, this brother of Joseph Smith trudged the byways of upper New York State in search of readers and listeners. His lonely mission, his determination to reach the honest in heart, and his pioneering pursuit of converts are expressed in this painting.

GOD SPEAKS IN MANY WAYS — This marble statue of a bird speaking into the ear of a boy shows man's close relationship to all God's creatures and suggests the need of a receptive, sensitive mind and heart as he learns from nature. When an artist creates a visual statement of a gospel concept, he does so because he is inspired by that concept. He also hopes that the viewer of his art will likewise find encouragement, edification, and inspiration.

CHASE SHEPARD, Artist
LORIN F. WHEELWRIGHT, Photographer

*The moral function of art
itself is to remove prejudice.*
— John Dewey

if sincerely expressed. This is his concept illustrated:

Christian perception gave another, a new direction to all human beings and therefore completely altered both the content and the significance of art. The Greeks could make use of Persian art, and the Romans could use Greek art. Or similarly, the Jews could use Egyptian art. The fundamental ideals were one and the same. Now the ideal was the greatness and prosperity of the Persians, now the greatness and prosperity of the Greeks, now that of the Romans. The same art was transferred to other conditions and served new nations. But the Christian ideal changed and reversed everything, so that as the Gospel puts it, "that which was exalted among men has become an abomination in the sight of God."

The ideal is no longer the greatness of Pharaoh or of a Roman emperor, not the beauty of a Greek or the wealth of Phoenicia, but humility, purity, compassion, love. The hero is no longer Dides, but Lazarus, the beggar. Not Mary Magdalene in the day of her beauty, but in the day of her repentance. Not those who acquire wealth, but those who dwell in catacombs and huts. Not those who rule over others but those who acknowledge no authority but God's. And the greatest work of art is no longer a cathedral of victory with statues of conquerors, but the representation of the human soul so transformed by love, that a man who is tormented and murdered yet pities and loves his persecutors.

Therefore, the subject matter of Christian art is of a kind that feeling can unite men with God and with one another. . . . The expression, "unite men with God and with one another" is that which unites all without exception.

. . . It must not transmit feelings accessible only to a man educated in a certain way or only to an aristocrat or a merchant or only to a Russian or a native of Japan or a Roman Catholic or a Buddhist, and so on, but it must transmit feelings accessible to everyone. Only art of this kind can, in our time, be acknowledged to be good art worthy of being chosen out from all the rest of art and encouraged.[9]

Tolstoy grants that, in addition to a perception of sonship to God and brotherhood of man, there is another type of expression that unites all men: namely, the simple feelings of common life accessible to everyone without exception, "such as feelings of merriment, of pity, or cheerfulness, or tranquility, etc. Only these two kinds of feelings can now supply

19

material for art good in its subject matter." He condemned as bad art:

all ecclesiastical, patriotic, and exclusive pictures; and pictures representing the amusements and allurements of a rich and idle life; all so-called symbolic pictures in which the very meaning of the symbol is comprehensible only to those of a certain circle, and above all, pictures of voluptuous subjects, all that odious female nudity which fills all the exhibitions and galleries.[10]

Tolstoy outlines as one criterion of art that it "remains what it was and what it must be, nothing but the infection of one man or of others with the feelings experienced by the artist." John Dewey disagrees on this point. He says:

I can but think that much of what Tolstoy says about immediate contagion as a test of artistic quality is false, and what he says about the kind of material which can alone be communicated is narrow. But if the time span be extended, it is true that no man is eloquent save when some one is moved as he listens. Those who are moved feel, as Tolstoy says, that what the work expresses is as if it were something one had oneself been longing to express. Meantime, the artist works to create an audience to which he does communicate. In the end, works of art are the only media of complete and unhindered communication between man and man that can occur in a world full of gulfs and walls that limit community of experience.[11]

The chief difference between Dewey and Tolstoy is the place of subject matter. Dewey claims that subject matter of art is immaterial to the aesthetic expression. Tolstoy claims that subject matter is as important as the form in which it is expressed and that it is an essential means of uniting all men.

At Brigham Young University, our faculty and students have partisans in both camps. However, Tolstoy's concept of the religious criterion would probably have more advocates than would Dewey's concept. This is particularly true in dramatic arts, less true in vocal music, somewhat true in visual arts, and least true in instrumental music. A current trend is the bridging of the gap between the instrumental and consummatory values of religious art, not only at Brigham Young University but also throughout the Church. The author hopes to see it happen throughout the nation and the world because he strongly believes that men tend to become like the substance on which they feed. If the substance of their art expresses the brotherhood of man, they might become more brotherly; whereas, if their art stresses secular interests, they tend to become secular in spirit. In so doing, they could miss those tremendous drives toward spiritual values that have built Western civilization.

A NEED FOR RESTORATION — This drawing expresses the decay and fracturing of the gospel of Christ and portrays the need for restoration. This is done by selecting symbolic forms which I feel can convey these ideas to the viewer. These forms include the crucifix, symbolizing the Christian church after Christ. Also, bone and distorted Christ forms are used to give meaning to the distortion of the body of Christ, the church, and a need for restoration.

JAMES L. YOUNG, *Artist*

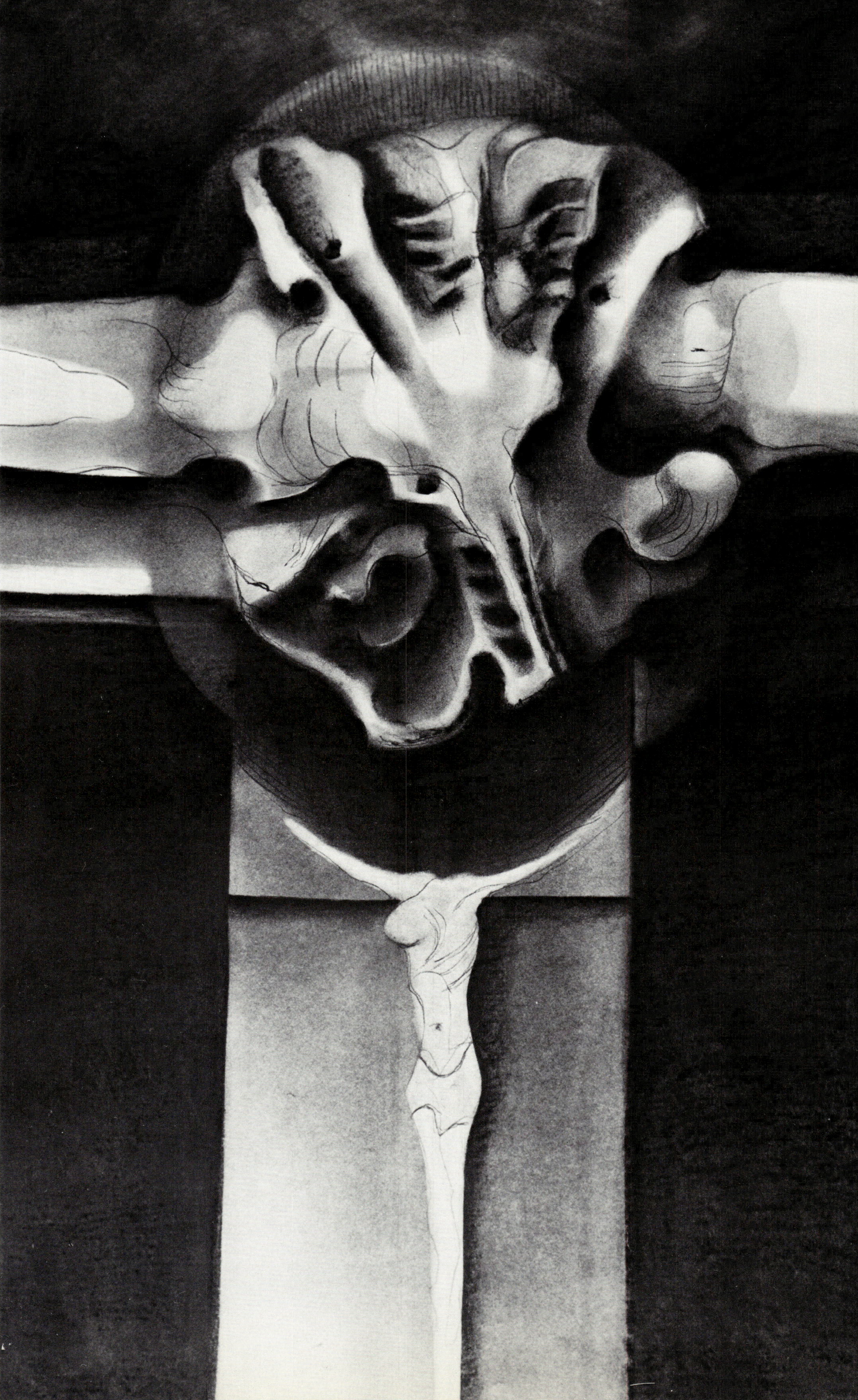

Tolstoy himself saw The Church of Jesus Christ of Latter-day Saints as a spearhead of religious motivation essential to a great forward movement. He once characterized Mormonism as the "American religion." To Dr. Andrew D. White, then United States ambassador to Germany, he said:

The Mormon people teach the American religion; their principles teach the people not only of Heaven and its attendant glories, but how to live so that their social and economic relations with each other are placed on a sound basis. If the people follow the teachings of this Church, nothing can stop their progress — it will be limitless. There have been great movements started in the past but they have died or been modified before they reached maturity. If Mormonism is able to endure, unmodified until it reaches the third and fourth generation, it is destined to become the greatest power the world has ever known.[12]

The College of Fine Arts and Communications is trying to develop consummatory value in expressing religious subjects. If successful, the arts of Brigham Young University will permeate not only the entire Church but the larger society of men. There is justification in such a hope, even from John Dewey. He says:

A consummatory object that is not also instrumental turns in time to the dust and ashes of boredom. The "eternal" quality of great art is its renewed instrumentality for further consummatory experiences.[13]

What Dewey is saying, of course, is that a work of art worthy of high esteem does not exhaust itself quickly, but as one returns to it time after time he finds a new interest and delight. There is no conflict between this aesthetic value and Mormon belief.

There is no one basis on which to judge all works of art, unless one assumes a fixed-value system. Art contains both instrumental and consummatory values. It is difficult to sustain either as a fixed system in the midst of a material society where cultures are in process of rapid change, or in an ecclesiastical society that believes in eternal progression.

It is the author's judgment that The Church of Jesus Christ of Latter-day Saints, which places its own expression of spiritual values at the apex of all values, is justified in using art instrumentally. This is based on the premise that men who appreciate and understand the spiritual values embodied in the Church experience a joy that transcends aesthetic pleasures.

Hath not the potter power over the clay, of the same lump to make one vessel unto honour, and another unto dishonour?

Romans 9:21

OVERCOMING THE FLESH,
David Mac Stevenson, Artist

21

MERRILL L. GOGAN, *Artist*

WOODEN SPOKES — Our pioneer heritage has provided a wealth of subject matter for all the arts. Dedication to a cause and the pioneer spirit can be depicted in unusual ways. **WOODEN SPOKES** directs the viewer to feel the hardships and the courage of those who may have used that old wagon wheel to transverse the long prairie of westward migration. This watercolor symbolizes one facet of our pioneer heritage.

SCHOOL'S OUT — Capturing the exuberance of children as they flee from the four walls of the schoolroom is the theme of this oil painting. For the older folk the picture is nostalgic of those good old days, when many early Mormon settlements had a one-room school. Younger people today know no such schools, and this picture helps them see the contrasts. For young and old, the common emotion of escape brings the generations together.

— Arthur H. King,
BYU Studies 11 (Autumn 1970): 48

It is up to us in our Church to educate ourselves to the point at which we can experience the best of art, and to begin with our children.

— Arthur H. King

GLEN HOPKINSON, *Artist*

However, as the people become increasingly sophisticated, the language of Mormon art, even though used in an instrumental way, must change to remain communicative. The pioneers of this change are the artists. Those who have sensitive, aesthetic natures and powers of expression — those who may see, feel, and create in idioms not identical with those of the past — need to be heard and viewed with humility and respect. Among their numbers might well be a Beethoven or a Michelangelo or a Rembrandt who may speak to many future generations of men. Although their accents may be strange to contemporary ears, their inspiration and sincerity can arise from the most fundamental rhythms and harmonies of religious conviction.

The role of the University is to preserve the artistic integrity of these sensitive people and to cultivate the disciplines essential to excellence of expression and communication. The University should inspire artists with concepts of universality that reach out to current and future generations. Artists so endowed can then communicate with "every nation, and kindred, and tongue, and people."[14] In so doing, art makes the distant glory more vivid and believable by making the present life brighter, happier, and more meaningful.

In conclusion, the author believes that art *is* a joy of man and an instrument of God. It is the power of one man to create in another feelings akin to his own. It serves God by leading men to those realms where joy incomprehensible awaits the righteous.

Art is personal. Those who never feel its intensity live in a cold, cold world. Those who do feel its glow are warmed through and through by the eternal fire.

LORIN F. WHEELWRIGHT

[1]2 Nephi 2:25.
[2]J. Spencer Cornwall, *A Century of Singing* (Salt Lake City: Deseret Book, 1958), p. 25.
[3]*Ibid.*, p. 117.
[4]*Ibid.*, p. 117.
[5]Monte B. Degraw, A Study of Representative Examples of Art Works Fostered by the Mormon Church with an Analysis of the Aesthetic Value of These Works," (unpublished Master's Thesis, Brigham Young University, 1959), pp. 25-26.
[6]Leo Tolstoy, *What Is Art?*, trans. by Aylmer Maude (New York: Oxford University Press, 1962), p. 231.
[7]John Dewey, *Art As Experience* (New York: Milton Balch Co., 1934), p. 190.
[8]Tolstoy, *op. cit.*, pp. 234-35.
[9]*Ibid.*, pp. 237-39.
[10]*Ibid.*, p. 248.
[11]Dewey, *op. cit.*, pp. 104-5.
[12]*Improvement Era*, Vol XLII, (Salt Lake City: Deseret Book, 1939), p. 94.
[13]John Dewey, *Art and Education* (Merion, Penn: The Barnes Foundation Press, 1929), pp. 7-8.
[14]Doctrine and Covenants 133:37.

SEEKING AESTHETIC EXPERIENCE

The teachings of Jesus offer a priority of motivation for all our actions including the quest for aesthetic experience. First is love of God (and all that is sacred and holy). Second is love of all men (with sensitive concern for their feelings). Third is love of self (with an obligation to share one's self through expression.) Love takes many forms which affect artistic creation; love of man for fellowman, love of man and woman for each other and for children, love of man for beauty, nature, truth, country, home; love of man for his own integrity and his work; and a host of others.

Love is a common heritage of man. It colors his personal relationships and shapes his hopes, fears, and joys — regardless of state and national boundaries or the expanse of time. It is a value that pervades Mormon art — particularly the art created by those who believe that the only art that will be called art in eternity will be created out of love for Christ, his doctrine and philosophy. They believe this simply because the powers of creation are centered in him alone, and man can only create when he puts himself in union with those powers.

Five Steps to Aesthetic Experience

In our experience with Mormon arts, or with any learning opportunity, each person begins where he is and moves upward and onward through distinct steps. Each step pushes us toward the next.

Let us explore these steps.

1. **Exposure**
   An event stirs our senses, making us aware of feelings caused by whatever has caught our attention.
2. **Meaning**
   We ask, "What is it?"
3. **Symbol**
   We attach a name, a label, a color, or some symbol with which we can think and weigh its properties.
4. **Value**
   We evaluate the meaning by deciding whether or not we like it, how it can serve or hurt us, and what we would pay to possess it or be rid of it.
5. **Response**
   We act or tend to act upon our determined value.

A measure of progress through these steps is increased ability to move from coarser to finer distinctions and from temporary to more lasting values. We may be experts in some things, but we are novices in most things. A teacher can expose, guide, and encourage, but each individual must ascend on his own power. Let us examine these steps in some detail.

Exposure (Is something catching my attention?)

Our first step in the cycle is confrontation with impressions. Each person "sees" the world through his own senses and from his own position. Because God made all men different, no two see alike — yet there are similarities in observation that make language and cultures possible. That we all move through periods of confusion is universal. As we examine wide variations of response, we ask, "Why do some see what others do not? How does man bring order out of chaos?"

A case is reported of a person who had been blind from birth. By surgery his sight was established, and he "saw" the world for the first time. When asked how it looked to him, he reported that all was a confusion of colors and blobs. He said that before he could really "see" he would have to learn to identify colors and distinguish forms. What others could take for granted, he must study and analyze until he learned distinguishing characteristics.

The emergence of Helen Keller from her prison of darkness came in the form of a teacher who untangled the chaos of her mind. Miss Keller described her coming in the summer of 1887 as "deliverance."

Thus I came up out of Egypt and stood before Sinai, and a power divine touched my spirit and gave it sight, so that I beheld many wonders. And from the sacred mountain I heard a voice which said, "Knowledge is love and light and vision."[1]

As our perceptions acquire discipline, we change from those who look but see not to those who see and understand. It is possible to find order in chaos, but we need discipline. Those who have "seen" and "heard" can often help us, especially when we stand in the presence of highly abstract or impressionistic art or attempt to untangle the "noise" of dissonant music.

Since our perception of art, music, and literary work begins with exposure, we must seek full communication for full enjoyment. Joy or displeasure arises directly from the aesthetic quality — commonly expressed as the beauty or ugliness — of this exposure. Best exposure can occur in the presence of original art works, such as an actual painting, a live musical performance, or live drama. For practical reasons, originals are not always available; therefore, we strive for reproductions as close to originals as possible. Hence, when phonograph recordings or tapes are played, they should be heard

AT SINEWAVA — I believe God, our Creator, is the greatest artist of all. The world and everything upon it stand as a testimony to him. We have been told that through our labors we can become as he is. I am striving through my art work to become more like God, to create after his creations, to become more sensitive to his creations. As with all of my art work, At Sinawava is my attempt to represent part of our beautiful world as I see and feel it; I hope that by so doing I may draw a little closer unto God.

KENT P. GOODLIFFE, *Artist*

through a sound system that is truly high fidelity, so the tone quality, frequency range, and volume approximate the original. Printed reproductions of paintings should approximate the color values of the original. Readings of literary works should convey the inflections of voice that approximate artistic interpretation. No one should be content until he has touched, in some way, an original artistic creation.

Meaning (What is it?)

When we ask, "What is it?" we seek meaning. Differences of interpretation can lead to conflict, and we see such a storm whipping many families. Some "popular" songs contain texts that to the unsuspecting appear insipid at worst. But to the "rock generation," who tune in on their double entendre, the words are highly intelligible enticements to commit immoralities. When the hidden meaning becomes clear, parents often arise in anger against those who would corrupt their children. In this instance, meaning causes pain.

Discovering meaning usually brings joy. This experience awaits those who find new or expanded meaning in a work of art. It is the "aha" response when someone senses an understanding for the first time. After listening to a concert of songs sung in foreign languages, what a pleasure it is to hear "The Lord's Prayer" in one's native tongue. The text is so familiar that most singers seem to use good diction.

Symbols and Values   (What do I call it? What is it worth to me?)

These two steps are linked together because we usually experience them together. Music, for example, embodies many symbols and values. The human voice can communicate the sigh of love or the cry of heartbreak. The human voice in opera rises and falls with each inflection. The words, important though they may be, are transported on wings of song that soar and fall in union with their meaning. So beautiful can be this marriage of music and meaning that one who does not know the language can follow the emotional significance of the text by listening to the music. The quality of voice and the harmonic support supply symbolic meaning. A cry of ecstasy or of pain needs no translation when artistically expressed. However, the full import of the music grows as one understands the text. The expanding circle moves onward with each added perception.

Our liking or disliking of symbol-meanings happens so quickly that most people are unaware of its nature. A word has little value in itself. Yet, the mind does seek a value for a word, and the two are inseparably linked. This bond of word and value is dramatically told by Helen Keller in her autobiography. One must feel again her emotions of frustration, insight, and joy to sense the significance of symbols in her life. The bridge from meeting words in early childhood to maturity is clearly shown by comparing chapters 4 and 20 of her autobiography. When viewing the different levels of experience represented in these two chapters, one senses the many learning steps that Miss Keller must have experienced as she matured.

Contrast this excerpt from childhood with her mature expression.

Miss Sullivan had tried to impress it upon me that "m-u-g" is *mug* and that "w-a-t-e-r" is *water*, but I persisted in confounding the two. In despair she had dropped the subject for the time, only to renew it at the first opportunity. I became impatient at her repeated attempts and, seizing the new doll, I dashed it upon the floor. I was keenly delighted when I felt the fragments of the broken doll at my feet. Neither sorrow nor regret followed my passionate outburst.[2]

. . . I have learned many things. . . . One of them is the precious science of patience, which teaches us that we should take our education as we would take a walk in the country, leisurely, our minds hospitably open to impressions of every sort. Such knowledge floods the soul unseen with a soundless tidal wave of deepening thought. "Knowledge is power." Rather, knowledge is happiness, because to have knowledge — broad, deep knowledge — is to know true ends from false, and lofty things from low. To know the thoughts and deeds that have marked man's progress is to feel the great heart-throbs of humanity through the centuries; and if one does not feel these pulsations a heavenward striving, one must indeed be deaf to the harmonies of life.[3]

As one probes his own mind for value, he might weigh the meaning of dramatic tragedy to determine the value it holds for him. In Shakespeare's *Hamlet*, the prince of Denmark finds no resolution of his mother's sin or his uncle's crimes, except in death. In searching for value, one might ask himself, "What does it profit a man to cheapen love? Why does the human heart recoil at falsehood, betrayal, and hypocrisy? Does life always have a happy ending? Why does tragedy make us weigh ultimate values?"

Response

When we experience a work of art that moves us to higher levels of understanding and creates new awareness of spiritual values, what do we do about it? Do we act to gain further experience so that learning might continue onward and upward in larger circles of awareness?

As we seek further adventures in the world of the aesthetic, we might search for answers to these questions:

1. How does a work of art help us see life more clearly?

2. How does a work of art help us face problems vicariously and with empathy for those who face them in reality?

3. How does a work of art help us discover specific values that have existed previously only as generalities?

Paul Tillich gives insight to such an inquiry:

Seeing means more than the creation of a world. When we see we unite with what we see. Seeing is a kind of union. As poetry has described it, we drink colors and forms, forces and expressions. They become part of ourselves. They give abundance to the poverty of our loneliness. Even when we are unaware of them they stream into us; but sometimes we notice them and welcome then and desire more of them.[4]

LORIN F. WHEELWRIGHT

---

[1]Helen Keller, *The Story of My Life* (New York: Dell Publishing Co., 1967), p. 32.
[2]*Ibid.*, pp. 33-34.
[3]*Ibid.*, pp. 94-95.
[4]Paul Tillich, *The New Being* (Scribners, 1955), p. 128.

EDWARD MARYON, *Artist*

DIVINE CREATION

Prior to gaining an understanding of man's artistic works, one really needs to study God's creations. With the advent of space travel, man now sees the world as a wondrous creation in the sky. In this article we shall compare this new vision with that of Renaissance and contemporary scientists and with the poetic insight of an early Mormon poet, Parley P. Pratt.

Oasis in Space

On Christmas Eve of 1968, voices from outer space echoed the majestic phrases of Genesis and thrilled every believer of God's holy word. All men soared to that lofty seat in the sky where each could see his earth revolving in its glory, a masterpiece of creation, formed by the Almighty.

Poetic declamation filled the hearts of those in the space capsule and those at home. About halfway to the moon, Frank Borman spoke:

I certainly wish that we could show you the earth. It is a beautiful, beautiful view with predominantly blue background . . . huge covers of white clouds.[1]

From 200,000 miles out, Lt. James Lovell, Jr., reported his impressions:

The earth is now passing through my window. It's about as big as the end of my thumb. Waters are all sort of a royal blue; clouds, of course, are bright white. The reflection off the earth is much greater than the moon. The land areas are generally sort of dark brownish to light brown. What I keep imagining is, if I were a traveler from another planet, what would I think about the earth at this altitude? Whether I think it would be inhabited?

GREAT WHITE THRONE — **Towering above the canyon floor of Zion National Park is this sheer monolithic mass, 2740 feet high. It is a landmark of sandstone and limestone. Its weathered face reveals centuries of sculpturing by the forces of nature. Evident are strata of windswept sands piled high in some ancient desert then overlaid by sedimentary deposits beneath a vast inland sea. Later came a continuous vertical thrust against the powerful erosion of atmosphere and water. By such a process, this dramatic work of nature's carving has come into being. At the dedication of this spot as a national park, a speaker proclaimed, with arms outstretched to the impressive red walls of Zion Canyon, "On this cliff I would write G - O - D, Great - Out - Doors." Our national parks preserve such masterworks. But one needs search no further for evidence of intelligent design in nature than the nearest leaf. In a most impressive display of creativity, the Almighty has shaped every green leaf to perform its photosynthesis and to embody a unique design among myriad species — all with infinite variations on a single theme. Such virtuosity humbles the most ambitious of human artists and challenges man to aspire to his eternal creative potential.**

On the ninth revolution of the moon, the crew spoke of what they saw and felt:

Borman: "The moon is a different thing to each one of us. . . . My own impression is that it's a vast, lonely, forbidding type of existence, a great expanse of nothing, that looks rather like clouds and clouds of pumice stone. It certainly would not appear to be a very inviting place to live or work."

Lovell: "Frank, my thoughts are very similar. The vast loneliness of the moon up here is awe-inspiring, and it makes you realize just what you have back there on earth. *The earth from here is a grand oasis to the big vastness of space.*"

Borman: "The sky is pitch black and the moon is quite light. The contrast between the sky and the moon is a vivid dark line."

Lovell: "Actually, I think the best way to describe this area is a vastness of black and white, absolutely no color."

Then Anders said, "For all the people back on earth, the crew of Apollo 8 has a message that we would like to send to you:

In the beginning God created the heaven and the earth. And the earth was without form, and void; and darkness was upon the face of the deep. And the spirit of God moved upon the face of the waters. And God said, Let there be light; and there was light. And God saw the light, that it was good: and God divided the light from the darkness . . . and God saw that it was good.

"And from the crew of Apollo 8, we pause with good night, good luck, a Merry Christmas, and God bless all of you — all of you on the good earth."[2]

Archibald MacLeish responded with these

SAINT GEORGE TEMPLE FROM BLOOMINGTON HILLS — Art work of a purely representational nature can leave the inner forces untapped. The spirit, essence or real meaning of a person or a painting is more internal than a visual veneer. This painting is no flimsy crust. The dynamic, dark undulations of the terrain stir our own rhythmic forces and speak of the powerful matrix of the earth's creation, of nature's vibrant and pulsating aliveness, of dimensions the mind can hardly fathom — yet, in the center of this caldron of physical energy the temple's spiritual dignity takes command. A Mormon temple is more than brick and mortar, so is Mathew's work. The sky is less cloud than an electrical burst that charges the heavens with forces to equal the landscape. The ground is less rocks and weeds than the ruggedness of the West itself. Then there is another dimension the artist has achieved higher than these expressionistic goals — he has organized the strong linear rhythms, the dramatic light and dark patterns, the intensified colors, and the spatial qualities of the sky and cupped valley into an orchestration of an aesthetic emotion for those who are tuned.

CONAN E. MATHEWS, *Artist*

words: "To see the earth as it truly is, small and blue and beautiful in that eternal silence where it floats, is to see ourselves as riders on the earth together, brothers on that bright loveliness in the eternal cold — brothers who know now they are truly brothers."[3]

A Mormon poet, Parley P. Pratt, expressed his wonder at the earth and the universe:

Boundless infinitude of time, and space,
And elements eternal! Who can trace
Earth with its treasures, Heaven with its spheres,
Time's revolutions, eternity's years?
But what are all these, when measured by thee,
But marks on thy dial, or motes on thy sea?
. . . .
What a vastness of design!
What display of wisdom!
What a field of labor in execution, do the works of
     creation
Present to the contemplative mind![4]

A Gift from God to Man

Scriptures ring with the beneficence of our Creator in making his gift of such an abode to man. The Lord has said:

Yea, all things which come of the earth, in the season thereof, are made for the benefit and the use of man, both to please the eye and to gladden the heart;

Yea, for food and for raiment, for taste and for smell, to strengthen the body and to enliven the soul.

And it pleaseth God that he hath given all these things unto man; for unto this end were they made to be used with judgment, not to excess, neither by extortion.

And in nothing doth man offend God, or against none is his wrath kindled, save those who confess not his hand in all things, and obey not his commandments.

Behold this is according to the law and the prophets.[5]

The gift of this earth is not appreciated by all men, neither is the Giver. To rectify man's past abuse of the earth, political forces are gathering to clean humanity's nest and tidy this planet as a dwelling place. Man is alarmed at the defacing of God's handiwork. Such defilement is abhorrent to those who love God and his creations. But to men who, in their atheism, declare God is dead, irreverence for both the structure and the Architect go hand in hand. Men who would destroy the Hand also destroy the handiwork.

THE SEA OF GALILEE — Water is a fascinating photographic subject because of its ever changing texture and highly reflective surface. At Galilee I found these qualities with the added dimension of religious feeling. These ripples, with highlight and shadow in close juxtaposition, not only reflect a quality of aliveness but also symbolize the highlights and shadows of those who gathered here, believing or doubting him who taught "peace, be still." Jesus walked on these waves, and Peter, wavering, began to sink. All of these events and more are reflected in this small lake which today continues to contrast the peace of a calm horizon against the turmoil of a troubled sky.

LORIN F. WHEELWRIGHT, *Photographer*

Nihilism is being seen as a direct result of atheism; wise men see that this negativism "sums up the situation of the era." Such is the observation of Martin Buber, the late Jewish philosopher, whose voice speaks as an Old Testament prophet in a modern wilderness. Buber describes man's blindness as an "eclipse of God."

Eclipse of the light of heaven, eclipse of God — such indeed is the character of the historic hour through which the world is passing. . . . An eclipse of the sun is something that occurs between the sun and our eyes, not in the sun itself . . . when, as in this instance, something is taking place between heaven and earth, one misses everything when one insists on discovering within earthly thought the power that unveils the mystery.[6]

Buber relates man's concept of God directly to his behavior and makes an eloquent plea for love of God, the reality, and not of God merely as a philosophical concept. He cites the writing of Pascal, the famous mathematician, who carried — sewn into the lining of his garment — the words "God of Abraham, God of Isaac, God of Jacob — not of the philosophers and scholars."[7] It was a personal God whom Abraham loved. It was this love that Pascal said was "the entire religion of the Jews."[8]

Our interest is to know God through his creations and to see what a "marvelous work and a wonder" he has wrought. Such inquiry leads to observations of scientists who see more

ABSTRACT STILL LIFE — "If there is anything virtuous, lovely, or of good report or praiseworthy, we seek after these things." This particular painting was created to demonstrate the technique of rearranging still life objects into a semiabstract composition and rendering them in an inventive method of approach. I chose the technique of crinkled butcher paper and ink batik which, to my knowledge, is original with me.

FLOYD V. CORNABY, *Artist*

clearly than others the relationships of matter. Their observations extend our own beyond visible horizons. Through their eyes we can see God's glory wherever we look. This glory has inspired poets, artists, and musicians, whose works invite us to explore with them more fully through the arts.

A Grand Design — an Everlasting Polyphony

Copernicus (1473-1543) and Kepler (1571-1630) observed the earth in relation to the solar system and witnessed in it a divine design.

Copernicus speaks of "the machinery of the world, which has been built for us by the Best and Most Orderly Workman of all." He said, "I finally discovered by the help of long and numerous observations that if the movements of the other wandering stars are correlated with the circular movement of the Earth, . . . that nothing can be shifted around in any part of them without disrupting the remaining parts and the universe as a whole."[9]

In his introduction to Book One, *On the Revolutions of the Heavenly Spheres,* he states:

Among the many and varied literary and artistic studies upon which the natural talents of man are nourished, I think that those above all should be embraced and pursued with the most loving care which have to do with things that are very beautiful and very worthy of knowledge. Such studies are those which deal with the godlike circular movements of the world and the course of the stars, their magnitudes, distances, risings and settings, and the causes of other appearances in the heavens; and which finally explicate the whole form. For what could be more beautiful than the heavens which contain all beautiful things? . . . For who, after applying himself to things which he sees established in the best order and directed by divine ruling, would not through diligent contemplation of them and through a certain habituation be awakened to that which is best and would not wonder at the Artificer of all things, in Whom is all happiness and every good? For the divine Psalmist surely did not say gratuitously that he took pleasure in the workings of God and rejoiced in the works of His hands, unless by means of these things as by some sort of vehicle we are transported to the contemplation of the highest Good.[10]

MORMON FESTIVAL CONCERT — An Easter Fireside concert involving more than 10,000 performers and 10,000 members of the audience featured the singing of "Oh, Cruel Thorns" (see pages 66-67) and "O Love, That Glorifies Thy Son" (see page 72). This finale to the Fourth Mormon Festival of Arts was the first musical concert to be held in the new Marriott Center.

29

FAMILY AT THE BEACH — This photo expresses family unity and love. It has a spiritual mood because of the setting and the flight of the bird (which signifies many Mormon values). I am strongly in favor of the old patriarchal family system in which leadership, strength, and a cohesion are firmer than all the peer groups of youth.
DON O. THORPE, *Photographer*

Johannes Kepler formulated three basic laws of planetary motion that led him to compare the solar system with music.[11] In his treatise entitled *Harmonies of the World* he related the movements of the planets to the major and minor scales. He arrived at a conclusion defining multiple movements as a quality of creation.

The movements of the heavens are nothing except a certain everlasting polyphony. . . . Hence it is no longer a surprise that man, the ape of his Creator, should finally have discovered the art of singing polyphonically . . . which was unknown to the ancients, namely in order that he might play the everlastingness of all created time in some short part of an hour by means of an artistic concord of many voices and that he might to some extent taste the satisfaction of God the Workman with His own works, in that very sweet sense of delight elicited from this music which imitates God.[12]

Rocks brought back by our astronauts stir our wonder about the moon's formation. Several theories are currently being examined.

1. The moon was formed at about the same time as the earth, probably out of the same gases in the solar system.

2. The moon was wrenched from the earth — possibly from what is now the Pacific Ocean — and reformed to become a permanent satellite of the earth.

3. Wandering by the earth from some distant birthplace in the solar system, the moon was captured by earth's gravity.[13]

The second of these theories has inspired Rachel Carson to project an imaginative account in *The Sea around Us.* She speaks as a poet as well as a scientist. Although recent Apollo flights indicate that the moon's origin is becoming less mysterious, the beauty of her writing makes plausible a theory which may or may not survive forthcoming lunar geological evidence.

The next time you stand on a beach at night, watching the moon's bright path across the water, and conscious of the moon-drawn tides, remember that the moon itself may have been born of a great tidal wave of earthly substance, torn off into space. And remember that if the moon was formed in this fashion, the event may have had much to do with shaping the ocean basins and the continents as we know them.

There were tides on the new earth, long before there was an ocean. In response to the pull of the sun the molten liquids of the earth's whole surface rose in tides that rolled unhindered around the globe, and only gradually slackened and diminished as the earthly shell cooled, congealed and hardened.

Those who believe that the moon is a child of the earth say that during an early stage of the earth's development something happened that caused this rolling, viscid tide to gather speed and momentum and to rise to unimaginable heights. Apparently the force that created these greatest tides the earth has ever known was the force of resonance, for at this time the period of the solar tides had come to approach, then equal, the period of the free oscillation of the liquid earth.

And so every sun tide was given increased momentum by the push of the earth's oscillation, and each of the twice-daily tides was larger than the one before it.

Physicists have calculated that, after 500 years of such monstrous, steadily increasing tides, those on the side toward the sun became too high for stability and a great wave was born away and hurled into space.

But immediately, of course, the newly created satellite became subject to physical laws that sent it spinning in an orbit of its own about the earth.

This is what we call the moon.[14]

The grand design of creation, as revealed by God, has stripped from the mind of man the mysticism and false theology "which have for ages shrouded the world in the sable curtains of a long and dreary night."[15] The gift of this design to man as a dwelling place and as a model of creative power is evidence of God's love of man and his concern for man's eternal life.

Infinite Truth

Parley P. Pratt states these "self-evident and incontrovertible facts":

1. There has always existed a boundless infinitude of space.

2. Intermingled with this space there exist all the varieties of elements, properties, or things of which intelligence takes cognizance; which elements or things taken together compose what is called the Universe.

3. The elements of all these properties of things are eternal, uncreated, self-existing. Not one particle can be added to them by creative power. Neither can one particle be diminished or annihilated.

4. These eternal, self-existing elements possess in themselves certain inherent properties or attributes in a greater or less degree; or, in other words, they possess intelligence adapted to their several spheres.[16]

Creative Significance of Art

In Genesis majestic phrases tell us that God made light, water, earth, grass, stars, moving creatures, and man. "And it was very good." As one listens to these biblical phrases and to the sounds of thunder, rain, rushing water, wind, and waves, they reveal God as an Almighty Sculptor.

Devout Mormons find great inspiration in nature. They see the work of a Master Designer everywhere evident. From such inspiration comes a flood of artistic expression that is more a paean of thanksgiving for God's gifts than a cry of alarm at man's desecration of those gifts. Some critics view Mormon landscape painters as living in another age and insensitive to current issues. This is superficial. Actually, the sincere landscape artist of today who looks with a spiritual eye to see glory in God's handiwork is free from the very inhibitions that limit some artists to ashcan views of the world. This viewpoint is based on a teaching of Joseph Smith: "If men do not comprehend the character of God, they do not comprehend themselves."[17] In sum, to understand man's artistic works, one really needs to comprehend God's creations.

LORIN F. WHEELWRIGHT

[1]The three astronauts in Apollo 8 mission were Frank Borman, James Lovell, and William Anders.
[2]Lt. Gen. Sam C. Phillips, USAF, "A Most Fantastic Voyage," *National Geographic,* May 1969, pp. 593-631. (Phillips is Apollo Program Director, NASA.)

VISION — **This painting is the result of a lengthy absorption I have had in the visualization of the plan of salvation and the relationships probably enjoyed by families prior to and following mortality. It evolved from a mortal family, however, and the baby is symbolized by showing only its face making for me a composition more satisfactory in content as well as form.**

TREVOR SOUTHEY, *Artist*

[3]Archibald MacLeish.
[4]Parley P. Pratt, *Key to Theology* (Liverpool: John Henry Smith, 1882), pp. 43, 56.
[5]D&C 59:18-22.
[6]Martin Buber, "Eclipse of God," in *Great Ideas Today* (Encyclopedia Britannica, Inc., 1967), p. 323.
[7]*Ibid.,* p. 333.
[8]*Great Books,* XXXIII, 280.
[9]Nicolaus Copernicus, *On the Revolutions of the Heavenly Spheres,* in *Great Books,* XVI, 508.
[10]*Ibid., p. 510.*
[11]Kepler's three laws:
1. All planets move in elliptical orbits having the sun as one focus (the law of orbits).
2. A line joining any planet to the sun sweeps out equal areas in equal times (the law of areas).
3. The square of the period of any planet above the sun is proportional to the cube of the planet's mean distance from the sun (the law of periods).
[12]*Great Books,* XVI, 1048.
[13]*U.S. News and World Report,* January 19, 1970, pp. 28-29.
[14]Rachel L. Carson, *The Sea around Us* (Mentor), p. 10.
[15]Pratt, p. 43.
[16]*Ibid.,* p. 44.
[17]Joseph F. Smith, *Teachings of the Prophet Joseph Smith,* Deseret Book, 1971, p. 343.

MAN CREATES IN THE IMAGE OF GOD

Latter-day Saints believe man is created with the capacity to become godlike. In his brief life on planet Earth, man is exposed to physical reality, to spiritual experiences, and to aesthetic design. From these experiences he perceives, symbolizes, derives meaning, values his meanings, and acts. As he ponders the gift of the earth, he is inspired to compose — in his finite way — echoes of the infinite. He struggles with the elements around him to form and communicate what he sees and feels. Man's creations parallel the Creator's designs when he employs the same principles that God has exemplified in his handiwork. When these forms approach perfection, touched by the unique individuality of a man's intelligence, we call them "works of art."

Aesthetic Principles Unite Man and God

From a study of divine revelation, physical discovery, and aesthetic expression, we see evidence of certain unifying principles. These principles show how man can create in patterns set before him in the universe by the great Creator himself. They serve as guides to development of the creative process — a process that man must master to achieve godliness and godhood. As one might know a parent through his children, so might we learn to understand how God creates by learning how man creates. These principles offer an approach to such a study. The examples cited aim to explore, with imagination, the world about us and to penetrate the infinite creative powers planted deeply within man.

Flagrant violations of these principles shift art experiences from the enjoyable to the annoying. Refinement and skill in their application invariably identify superior from inferior art and help the viewer understand the difference. Fifteen principles are listed on subsequent pages. These are cited here by number in reference to specific illustrations. These principles unite basic concepts of religion, science, and aesthetics. They express common truth in these varied approaches to life.

PILLAR OF TULA — Pillars such as these were used to support the roof of a building that was on top of the pyramid-temple located at Tula, Mexico, some sixty miles north of Mexico City. This was the headquarters of the Toltec nation and reflects the cultures of centuries of living prior to its time. This pillar was thought to be built about A.D. 800-900.

PAUL R. CHEESMAN, *Photographer*

The Rhythm of Dark to Light

Basic units of design employ twos and threes — that is a basic principle of creative form. As we study the phenomenon of *two*, we see it evidenced in infinite forms wherever strong contrasts are evident. One of the most common in nature is night and day. Many musical compositions have been composed to commemorate the different moods and transitions from one to another of these contrasting experiences. Dawns and sunsets have intrigued painters, poets, architects, and others who have created aesthetic symbols of emergence. Let us examine an example of music that transports us from dark to light.

The Morning Breaks

"The Morning Breaks; the Shadows Flee" is a hymn by Parley P. Pratt, sung to a hymn tune by George Careless. Both of these men were first-generation Mormons. The song's first line — in both content and form — expresses the duality of life, the basic binary form that is so native to man and his works. "The morning breaks; the

Man's imagination deals with the supernatural and projects forms of his idealized expectations. Such forms can express deep-seated anxieties and fears as well as high ideals and concepts of power. In all, man's works reveal how he expresses "I am." LORIN F. WHEELWRIGHT

In art . . . we discern eternity looking through time, the Godlike rendered visible.

— Carlyle

Supposing I have a lump of clay . . . I have to turn it into 50 or 100 shapes before I get it into a jug. . . . How many shapes do you suppose you are put into before . . . you become perfect and sanctified to enter into the celestial glory of God?

— Heber C. Kimball

CERAMICS — The potter craftsman not only chooses his tools but he himself becomes the tool of his idea; he brings together what he wants and plans with what he can do and knows, what he can see and touch. He chooses and organizes size, shape, methods, materials, and techniques for this one particular circumstance. He orders diversity toward one aim and out of chaos grows form.

It is a known fact that the more one learns, the more remains to be learned. It seems that a person will never quite reach that total view to which he aspires. But is that not the best of life? One never reaches an end, one only reaches death. But as one tries and searches, his capacities seem to multiply and grow. Isn't this true of our testimony of the truthfulness of The Church of Jesus Christ of Latter-day Saints?

MAX D. WEAVER, *Artist*

33

shadows flee" are two phrases. They contrast with "Lo! Zion's standard is unfurled." However, both of these longer phrases may be considered Part A of the hymn; Part B becomes the balance, which reads: "The dawning of a brighter day [repeated] Majestic rises on the world." As a formal structure, the stanza might be diagrammed thusly:

A	B
a, b	c, (c) d

(See the reprint of this hymn for a structural analysis.)

Musically, the hymn tune in Part A has two phrases of four measures. In Part B, one phrase is repeated, making a total of three phrases of four measures. So, in total, we have an A B form with A = 2 and B = 3. This illustrates the second principle: *Basic units of design employ twos and threes or their combinations.* This same basic structure is evident in the melody itself. Note that the meter is in 3:4, meaning three beats to a measure. In the first phrase the basic rhythm might be diagrammed like this:

The / morn - ing / breaks the / shad - ows / flee.

- / / - / / - / / - / /

Note that in each measure two beats are given to the first syllable of text. Note also that the overall design of the phrase consists of a repeated pattern in which the two beats of the first syllable contrast with the three beats of the measures — another evidence of *twos* and *threes* in combination.

In the second phrase the rhythm might be diagrammed like this:

Lo! Zi - on's / stan - dard / is un - / furl'd

/ / /   / /   - // - //-

Note that the first measure has three strong beats of equal stress and that the balance of the phrase uses the same pattern of 2-1 used in the first phrase. Here is a combination of three (beats) and three (measures) — the first measure setting a pattern of *threes* that is repeated in the balance of the three measures as a repetition, or more properly, as an extension of the first basic design.

This kind of analysis escapes most people because "they either like the music or they don't." But it is basic to understanding why they like it, whether they consciously realize its design elements or only sense them as a total experience.

This analysis also illustrates the twelfth principle: *That which appears simple becomes complex upon analysis.* This principle is essential for anyone who aspires to compose music. Unless he really knows how to shape basic musical elements, his work could easily violate the first principle: *All parts of creation are related; all parts belong to a whole.* Violation of this principle is the most common problem of the

The Morning Breaks; the Shadows Flee

Parley P. Pratt

George Careless

"The Morning Breaks; the Shadows Flee" appears on Mormon Arts Recording I included with this volume.

unskilled composer. Its violation leaves something disturbing to the listener. The story is told of an amateur composer who brought a page of his new symphony to Beethoven. After the great composer examined it, he said that it was filled with musical ideas; in fact, he asserted that there were more ideas on that one page than he himself had needed to write all his symphonies. The great composer's criticism was leveled at the amateur's lack of development of *one* idea. It is this development that marks a good composition in any of the arts and in all of nature. As one looks at a tree and studies its roots, trunk, limbs, branches, twigs, and leaves, he imme-

diately senses that the roots and limbs constitute a binary form of almost equal strength, joined by a trunk that holds the two parts together. Where the trunk is extended, it might be considered as a third part. So, a tree could be diagrammed like this:

roots	trunk	limbs
/	-	/
A	B	A

Or, if the limbs spread directly above the ground, as in some shrubs, the form would be:

roots	limbs
A	B

A further study of "The Morning Breaks" reveals that the imagery of the text follows the same basic binary form: cause and effect. The morning breaks (cause); the shadows flee (effect). Clouds disappear (cause); glory bursts (effect).

Not only does this hymn express a basic form of all creation, it does so with great beauty. We might ask, "Why did George Careless extend the B part to three phrases by repeating one of them? Why did he not keep it to two and have perfect symmetry?" This is like asking, "Why did God make five fingers instead of four?" The answer lies in ultimate purpose. All we can do is surmise, as we see in the fifteenth principle: *Man's imagination stretches his perception to infinite magnitudes.* God himself said, "For mine own purpose have I made these things. Here is wisdom and it remaineth in me." (Moses 1:31.) Everyone who creates moves in directions that only the imagination can comprehend. Explicit reasons usually fall short of a basic and natural reason that is inherent in man's (and God's) very nature. One might answer the first question and assume that George Careless used three phrases in the B part to extend the form and make it more impressive and that he did so to enhance the climactic character of his theme. Dawn seems to stretch and stretch, then suddenly burst in a glorious sunrise. This may have been his motive. It makes sense and is one way to rationalize a creative experience that probably

TIMPANOGOS — I stand in awe and gaze in wonder — I assume their power, yet am humbled in turn — I stand apart although a part — they tax my strength, yet heal my spirit — they lift me up above myself — these mountains. FLOYD E. BREINHOLT, *Artist*

was so inherent in the way the composer thought that he might not have been consciously aware of his own feeling for the form. However, such an assumption is not entirely safe because most composers of stature are deliberate in their shaping of material and do know why they do what they do.

This musical illustration demonstrates, in one instance, how the following principles apply to an art form. The reader is urged to apply them to many works in many media to test their validity.

UNIFYING PRINCIPLES

DIVINE REVELATION	PHYSICAL DISCOVERY	AESTHETIC EXPRESSION

1. All parts of creation are related: all parts belong to a whole.

DIVINE REVELATION	PHYSICAL DISCOVERY	AESTHETIC EXPRESSION
For as the body is one, and hath many members, and all the members of that one body, being many, are one body: so also is Christ. (1 Corinthians 12:12.)	The planets revolve around the sun, held in orbit by a balance of centrifugal force and gravity.	The instruments of a symphony orchestra play together in balance and harmony, united by a conductor and the score of a composer.

2. Basic units of design employ twos and threes or their combinations.

DIVINE REVELATION	PHYSICAL DISCOVERY	AESTHETIC EXPRESSION
In the beginning God created the heaven and the earth. (Genesis 1:1.) earth and seas (Genesis 1:10.) day and night (Genesis 1:14.) two great lights (Genesis 1:16.) male and female (Genesis 1:27.) [Two parts] . . . baptizing them in the name of the Father, and of the Son, and of the Holy Ghost. (Matthew 28:19.) And now abideth faith, hope, charity, these three . . . (Corinthians 13:13.) [Three parts]	The constant revolving of the earth in relation to the sun sustains a rhythm of day and night. [A pattern of two]	The accented beat of the drum sustains a dance in meters of twos, threes, or their combinations. [Twos and threes]

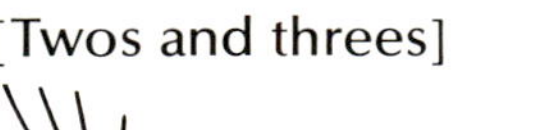

3. Identical parts are actually variations on a theme.

DIVINE REVELATION	PHYSICAL DISCOVERY	AESTHETIC EXPRESSION
And God made the beast of the earth after his kind, and cattle after their kind, and every thing that creepeth upon the earth after his kind: and God saw that it was good. (Genesis 1:25.)	Leaves of a tree appear similar but are not identical. They show infinite variations in details of shape, size, color, and weight.	No two violins in the orchestra, or voices in a choir, are identical. Slight differences enhance the ensemble.

4. All parts are in motion.

DIVINE REVELATION	PHYSICAL DISCOVERY	AESTHETIC EXPRESSION
And as one earth shall pass away, and the heavens thereof even so shall another come; and there is no end to my works, neither to my words. (Moses 1:38.)	The earth, which seems fixed, is constantly turning and its crust shifts within itself.	Curved lines and contrasting colors in a painting create the effect of a dynamic flow of forces.

5. Movement occurs in curved lines with accents and contra rhythms.

DIVINE REVELATION	PHYSICAL DISCOVERY	AESTHETIC EXPRESSION
Whatsoever the Lord pleased, that did he in heaven, and in earth, in the seas, and all deep places. He causeth the vapours to ascend from the ends of the earth; he maketh lightnings for the rain; he bringeth the wind out of his treasuries. (Psalms 135:6-7.)	The ocean undulates in ripples, waves, tides, and currents.	The plot of a drama moves from event to event with every word and gesture creating a flow of interaction.

DIVINE REVELATION	PHYSICAL DISCOVERY	AESTHETIC EXPRESSION

6. Equal forces create stability; unequal forces create movement.

Yea, though I walk through the valley of the shadow of death, I will fear no evil: for thou art with me; thy rod and thy staff they comfort me. (Psalms 23:4.) Behold, the day of the Lord cometh, cruel both with wrath and fierce anger, to lay the land desolate: and he shall destroy the sinners thereof out of it. (Isaiah 13:9.)	Land, sand, and snow lie motionless until moved by wind, gravity, or some other force. 	An arch suspends heavy stones aloft by distributing their weight equally onto supporting columns.

7. Many forces exist beyond man's sensory perception.

And by the power of the Holy Ghost ye may know the truth of all things. . . . deny not the power of God; for he worketh by power, according to the faith of the children of men, the same today, and tomorrow, and forever. (Moroni 10:5, 7.)	Radio waves pass through the human body without perceptible effect, but they can activate a tuned receiver. 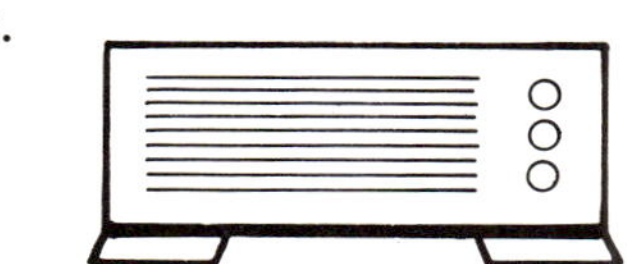	A marching band, some distance away, will appear to be out of step with the music because the sound waves are retarded by the invisible atmosphere whereas the light waves are not impeded.

8. Things change, but not God's being or his principles.

Return unto me and I will return unto you. . . . For I am the Lord, I change not. (Malachi 3:7, 6.) And God saw their works, that they turned from their evil way; and God repented of the evil, that he had said that he would do unto them; and he did it not. (Jonah 3:10.) For I know that God is not a partial God, neither a changeable being; but he is unchangeable from all eternity to all eternity. (Moroni 8:18.)	All elements can be converted to energy or light. Erosion constantly carves the face of the earth. 	A work of art is repeatedly seen as different by an individual because his own responsiveness changes throughout his lifetime. 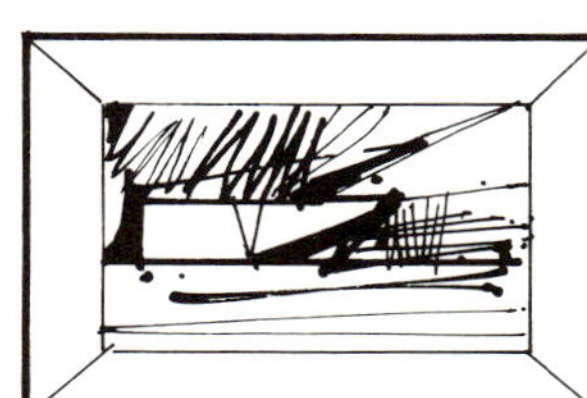

9. Time is measured by change.

One day is with the Lord as a thousand years, and a thousand years as one day. (2 Peter 3:8.) One man esteemeth one day above another: another esteemeth every day alike. (Romans 14:5.) But the day of the Lord will come as a thief in the night; in the which the heavens shall pass away with a great noise, and the elements shall melt with fervent heat, the earth also and the works that are therein shall be burned up. (2 Peter 3:10.)	The changed position of the earth in relation to the sun marks the passing of days and years. 	The tempo of music, dance, and drama is measured by the rate of change in direction of movement or the pulsation of beats. 

DIVINE REVELATION	PHYSICAL DISCOVERY	AESTHETIC EXPRESSION
10. Blind habit limits perception; new insight requires new vision.		
Therefore speak I to them in parables; because they seeing see not; and hearing they hear not, neither do they understand. . . . their ears are dull of hearing, and their eyes they have closed. (Matthew 13:13, 15.) In the last days, saith God, I shall pour out my Spirit upon all flesh: . . . and your young men shall see visions, and your old men shall dream dreams: . . . And I will show wonders in heaven above, and signs in the earth beneath; blood, and fire, and vapour of smoke; (Acts 2:17, 19.)	For centuries the sun "obviously" revolved around the earth. New observation brought new conception. 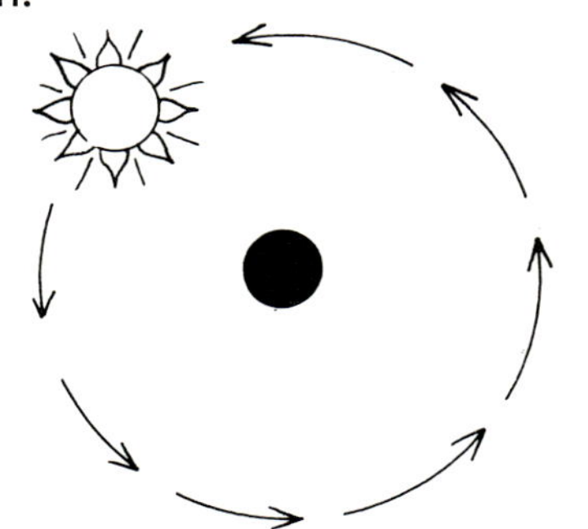	For centuries man perceived objects of equal size as equal whether near or far away. When he conceived perspective, he painted the same-sized objects in different sizes on his canvas to show distance. 
11. Freshness of viewpoint reduces man's fatigue and prolongs his interest.		
And it came to pass, when Jesus had ended these sayings, the people were astonished at his doctrine: For he taught them as one having authority, and not as the scribes. (Matthew 7:28-29.) I have compassion on the multitude, because they have been with me three days, and have nothing to eat. . . . So they did eat, and were filled. (Mark 8:2, 8.)	The sky becomes increasingly fascinating to the astronomer as he sees with more powerful optical telescopes, radio telescopes, sensitive photographic film, and computerized calculations.	Superior art works contain subtle relationships that become more and more interesting upon repeated contact and sharpened perception.
12. That which appears simple becomes complex upon analysis.		
[Jesus said] O ye hypocrites, ye can discern the face of the sky; but can ye not discern the signs of the times? (Matthew 16:3.) I will open my mouth in parables; I will utter things which have been kept secret from the foundation of the world. (Matthew 13:35.) O Lord, how great are thy works: and thy thoughts are very deep. (Psalms 92:5.)	The "original" elements consisted of earth, water, air, and fire. Now man has identified 103 distinct elements with precise atomic structure. 	A "simple" tune, when analyzed, becomes a sequence of tones of variable pitches, quality of sound, dynamics, and tendencies of movement.
13. Man feels a kinship with the earth by creating forms common to nature and himself.		
Ye are blessed of the Lord which made heaven and earth. The heaven, even the heavens, are the Lord's: but the earth hath he given to the children of men. (Psalms 115:15,16.) Ye are the salt of the earth. . . . Ye are the light of the world. . . . Consider the lilies of the field. . . . A good tree cannot bring forth evil fruit. (Matthew 5:13,14: 6:28; 7:18.)	Nature exemplifies qualities of light and darkness, weight and buoyancy, sparkle and dullness.	Man's music can whisper as the breeze or roar as the wind. Man dances lightly on his toes and heavily upon his soles. Man creates word pictures and paintings that soak up the light or glisten in the sun.

<table>
<tr><th>DIVINE REVELATION</th><th>PHYSICAL DISCOVERY</th><th>AESTHETIC EXPRESSION</th></tr>
</table>

14. Man synthesizes parts to create wholeness.

I say unto you, that every idle word that men shall speak, they shall give account thereof in the day of judgment. (Matthew 12:36.)

Jesus said unto him, Thou shalt love the Lord thy God with all thy heart, and with all thy soul, and with all thy mind. This is the first and great commandment. And the second is like unto it, Thou shalt love thy neighbour as thyself. On these two commandments hang all the law and the prophets. (Matthew 22:37-39.)

Man condenses many theories relating to matter and energy into one simple formula:

$$E = mc^2.$$

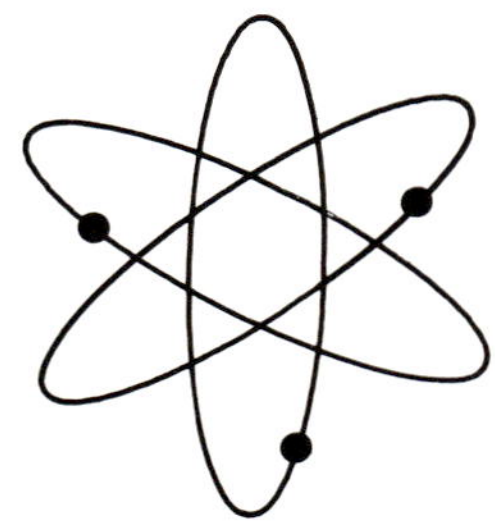

Man builds a temple to God to feel unity with his Creator when he views it, enters it, or contemplates its meaning.

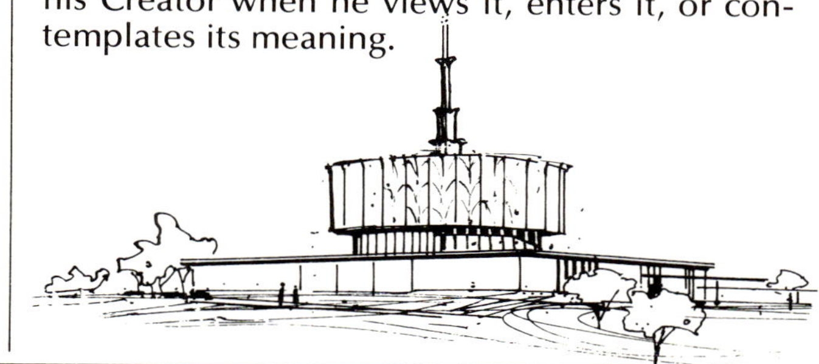

15. Man's imagination stretches his perceptions to infinite magnitudes.

Moses looked, and beheld the world upon which he was created; and Moses beheld the world and the ends thereof, and all the children of men which are, and which were created; of the same he greatly marveled and wondered. . . . And the Lord God said unto Moses: For mine own purpose have I made these things. Here is wisdom and it remaineth in me. . . . there are many worlds that have passed away by the word of my power. (Moses 1:8, 31, 35.)

From subatomic particles to stellar galaxies, man perceives creation as a vast extension of what he knows.

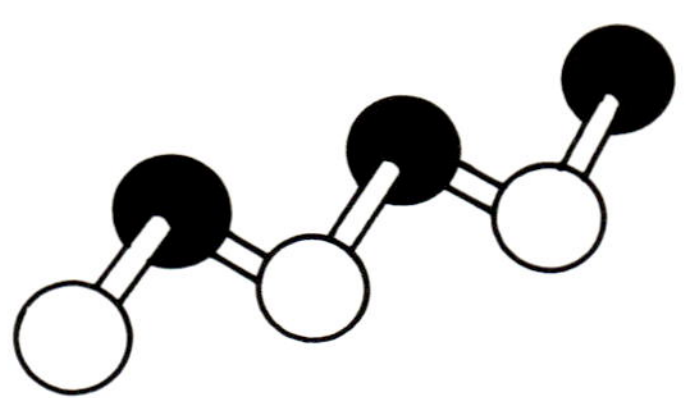

A drama reaches beyond the proscenium arch; a picture extends beyond the frame; words glow with new meaning when sung; and vibrating strings moan as devils or lilt as angels — all in the mind of man.

RED CANYON BUTTES — A fascinating phenomenon is the constant evidence in natural forms of the principle shown here: "Basic units of design employ two's and three's or their combinations."

LORIN F. WHEELWRIGHT, Author

ART EXPRESSES OPPOSITION IN ALL THINGS

For man to have joy and live more abundantly, he must understand the nature of opposing forces and how to deal with them. He must develop the discipline of making wise choices by knowing and feeling the consequences of those choices.

Art consists of designed expressions of opposing forces in forms that allow the artist to communicate with his fellowmen. Art may concern itself with idle pastimes that fill in the gaps of boredom with fascinating diversion, or it may deal with man's basic concerns. In either case it is designed to bring joy to man by helping him solve the puzzle, find the meaning, or discover the orderly design in what otherwise might remain a chaotic world. Sometimes the artist attempts no more than to use his expressive skill to help man see his world more clearly, feel it more intensely, and broaden his total awareness. Art grows in significance and stature when it deals with the vital concerns of man and helps him think more penetratingly about his choices. Art has greater value when it helps him intensify his perceptions of and feelings for the forces that shape his life. It reaches its greatest dimension when it affects all men and creates for them a system of values which make life more worth living.

Life would be meaningless without opposing forces. We are told explicitly in the Book of Mormon that "it must needs be, that there is an opposition in all things. If not . . . all things must be a compound in one . . . having no life . . . happiness nor misery, neither sense nor insensibility."[1] Art that is devoid of opposing forces is not art at all. It is precisely what this scripture says it is: a lifeless compound.

Each art form, in its own ways, deals with opposing forces. The beholder is drawn to art because of the "beautiful" way in which these forces work upon each other in a design that makes sense. The process of "working out"

FORCES OF OPPOSITION — Tragedy forces us to weigh ultimate values. The martyrdom of Joseph Smith, historically the greatest tragedy for Latter-day Saints, exemplifies the tremendous conflict of good and evil in the world. As we witness an artist's rendering of this traumatic event, we cannot help but sense the reality of the contrast between good and evil and recognize that the forces of opposition do exist.

GARY E. SMITH, *Artist*

the tensions becomes an exciting and pleasurable pursuit and leads to moments of ecstasy referred to by those who have known them as "aesthetic experiences." Such experiences are sometimes described as "chills going up and down my spine." Other descriptive words are *fascinated, spellbound, transported, elevated, captivated,* and *purified.*

The intensity of this aesthetic experience depends upon both the artist's genius and the beholder's receptivity. What may be one viewer's passion may be another's poison. Personal taste and background become selective factors, but probably equal in importance is the sensory acuity of the beholder. The color-blind or totally blind person would find color in painting far less significant than one who is highly endowed with vision. General intelligence in dealing with multiple abstractions also affects perception and leads to a differentiation of response, sometimes referred to as "levels of response." One quality of great art is its power to speak to the humble peasant or the sophisticated critic at each person's level of perception and understanding. The parables of Jesus illustrate this diversity of appeal. However, the Savior made clear that he did not intend that only the obvious meanings were his purpose. He strove for the more subtle and spiritual meanings and taught his disciples how to "tune in" on this level of understanding.

A comparable "tuning in" is needed to wring from great art its full value. Although men may be content to say, "I know what I like but don't ask me why!" such confessions are really the rationalizations of the lower levels of response. To rest content in ignorance is not a goal of life for the Latter-day Saint. Rather, he is challenged to become perfect in all things — to learn from out of the best books; to ponder in his heart; to seek, ask, and find. His ultimate goal is to become as all-knowing as his Creator, who designed all of the forms of nature in their infinite beauty and variety. He aspires to become qualified to equal these powers in his own eternal progress.

Such are the challenges and opportunities facing the sincere Latter-day Saint who not only studies the lower forms of God's creations but concentrates upon the highest form of all — man. The arts reveal man. Each in its own unique way expresses the opposition in all things that man faces and tries to resolve. Drama portrays the basic conflicts of man against man, man against fate, man against himself. Music expresses opposing forces by sounds of dissonance that struggle for consonance, by counter rhythms and melodies, by contrasting tempos and dynamic intensities, and by tonal structures that weave a fascinating design.

The visual arts pit masses against intensities of

WALLACE M. BARRUS, Photographer

color. Their lines often thrust, intersect, and disrupt a sense of belonging. Architecture struggles to overcome gravity and imbalance of parts within the whole by arches, pillars, cantilevers, and a host of techniques. In speech, ideas are pitted against each other, feelings are juxtaposed, logic and illogic are debated. Poems express intense personal feelings and insights that are unique to the poet. They reveal his inner ponderings of things, sensations, and meanings.

The skill of the artist is to lead his beholder into a microcosm of life's struggles and help him resolve them in a design that makes emotional sense — a sense of peace after the climax. He is a synthesist rather than an analyst. He fulfills his viewer's deep longing for order. In this function he parallels the theologian in religion. Some artists would presume to replace him, particularly those theologians who have lost their relevance to our society. But, in The Church of Jesus Christ of Latter-day Saints, the artist is a co-worker and ally of the theologian. He seeks ways to bring order out of chaos on principles of eternal truth. He is concerned with all dimensions of man and seeks to express his struggles to reveal the inevitable tie between cause and consequence as manifestation of divine law. Sometimes he leaves his problems well stated but unanswered.

The artist soon discovers that men differ widely in their values and resultant practices. Also, he discovers threads of common conviction running through myriad cultures. His desire to know all things drives him to explore these cultures and compare them to his own. The arts become his chief sources of knowledge because they reveal men's feelings, customs, and manner of relating one to another. For example, he sees Greek architecture, sculpture, drama and hears the poems of Homer and Virgil. These tell him how the Greeks thought and felt. He becomes, as it were, an ancient Greek himself — fighting for his country, thinking his philosophy, standing in his temples, witnessing the joys and sorrows of mankind. He discovers that the Greeks abhorred incest. He senses this horror more intensely by witnessing the drama of *Oedipus Rex.* He discovers his cultural genealogy, and his heart turns to his fathers; and through the arts, the fathers turn to him. But he also witnesses the philosophical belief of

---

DRAMATIC MOMENTS FROM W-2 FORM — This experiment in theatrical form explored, in voice, movement, and a plexiglas sculpture of the pre, present and post existence of the human family, man's relationship to eternity (top). It depicted the oppositional and successional forces of man's body and will as he relates to other men (center). And it surveyed the complexity of man's response to himself and the intricacies of his world (bottom). (see page 57)

these pagan ancestors which held that men are puppets manipulated by the gods for their own amusement, and he sees the futility of this religion. He sees great value in his own belief by comparing it with another. This weighing of ideas as expressed in the arts, also helps him recognize erroneous views in contemporary religions. In the process he expands his knowledge. His values grow, his living is more abundant, and his joy is more complete.

That such pursuit is desirable is expressed in our Thirteenth Article of Faith which commits us to the admonition of Paul — "We believe all things, we hope all things, we have endured many things, and hope to be able to endure all things. If there is anything virtuous, lovely, or of good report or praiseworthy, we seek after these things."[2] Such pursuit becomes essential for the Latter-day Saint who accepts belief in a personal God, faith, repentance, and baptism. It is essential to his temporal existence and to his eternal progress.

LORIN F. WHEELWRIGHT

[1] 2 Nephi 2:11
[2] Joseph Smith, "Articles of Faith"

If I were placed on a cannibal island and given the task of civilizing its people, I should straightway build a theatre for the purpose.

Brigham Young

DARK CONTINENT — This painting, produced several years after a poem by the same title, personifies the universal and ceaseless conflict between the forces of good and evil. Although the good, pathetically outnumbered, appears to be losing another battle, man still stubbornly and hopefully believes that truth will ultimately win the war. This struggle is indeed a sad and frightening spectacle, but when right is ruthlessly killed, as it often is, in a noble effort to do good (as in this particular instance in which William McChesney, "a 'heart of Africa' missionary affiliated with the worldwide evangelization crusade at Washington," meets a horrendous death with 206 others), it indeed becomes a tragedy that repeats once again the demise of the Savior.

ALEX B. DARAIS, Artist

C.C.A. CHRISTENSEN,
Mormon Artist

MORMON PANORAMA

An early convert to the Latter-day Saint Church, with very little formal art training, produced a significant series of paintings relating to the persecutions, hardships, and wanderings of the Saints. Carl Christian Anton Christensen was born in Copenhagen, Denmark, in November 1831. By the time he was eleven, he had already given some evidence of artistic talent. He was a poor boy, but several kind ladies took an interest in him and saw that he attended the best art schools of his native city. He was studying art in 1844, the year of the tragic murders of Joseph and Hyrum Smith. After becoming a member of The Church of Jesus Christ of Latter-day Saints, he and his wife pushed a handcart to the Salt Lake Valley where C.C.A., as he was known to fellow Mormons, completed his major work. He procured twenty-two pieces of heavy linen, each one eight by ten feet. In 1869 he began to paint significant incidents concerning the history of the Mormon Church. Some of these — such as the burning of the Nauvoo Temple, the death of Captain Fearnot, the raid by non-Mormons on Mormon settlements, and the thirteen-hundred-mile walk from Council Bluffs to the Salt Lake Valley — were part of his own personal experience. He completed all these pictures by 1890. But long before then, in 1878, he had sewn the first group of eight together, rolled them on a long wooden pole, and placed the whole package in his wagon. Then, using the pictures as illustrations for a lecture on Mormon history, he drove through the Utah country advertising his appearance as a lecturer on the Mormon story. C.C.A. died in Ephraim, Utah, in 1912, but much of his vitality and love of the gospel remains in the form of his paintings. The bright, clear colors; the vitality of the human figures; and the strength of the compositions give them a unique quality. At a time in the early history of American art, when paintings were somewhat academically and woodenly categorized as portraits, landscapes, and historics, Christensen accomplished a melding of the latter two into a vigorous style that proved superior to most of the painting of his time.

ALLEN CORNWALL, *Editor*

In September 1827, when Joseph Smith, the Mormon prophet, was 21 years old, an angel named Moroni delivered to him a set of golden plates which were a record of the early inhabitants of the American continent. Joseph Smith's translation of the plates is the Book of Mormon. Here the artist depicts Joseph receiving the plates from the angel.

In late March 1832, near Kirtland, Ohio, when Joseph Smith was sleeping — after staying up most of the night with a sick child — a dozen men burst into the room, seized him, and dragged him into a field. There they tore off his clothes, beat and scratched him, and covered his bruised body with hot tar and feathers; nevertheless, he appeared at church the following day and calmly preached without any mention of the attack he had endured the previous evening.

Gentiles, the Mormon name for non-Mormons, burned barns, tore down cabins, destroyed crops, and attacked Mormon families with extreme violence. Nonetheless, the Mormons clung to their beliefs with tenacity and fought back with dogged determination. Some of their neighbors expressed great bitterness against them, and a hostile folklore began to assert itself. Mormon-haters resented the Mormon way of life and the Mormon claim that Joseph Smith was a true prophet of the Lord.

When mobbers planned to destroy Zion's camp, their leader declared that if he did not get Joseph Smith and his army in two days the buzzards might pick his bones. Soon their boat leaked. The leader said, "If we don't strip and swim for dear life, we will soon be in hell." A companion replied, "I'd rather go to hell with my clothes on than land naked." Of the mobbers shown above, seven were drowned.

Because of the persecutions, Joseph Smith considered leading his followers westward toward an untroubled land where they might live in peace and happiness — a western land which the Lord had made known to him in a revelation. The gentile neighbors of the Mormons in Missouri were jealous of the successful farming communities they developed, the fruitfulness of their plowed fields, and their thrift and industry.

The expedition sent to disperse a group threatening the Mormons in Far West, Missouri, and to free prisoners being held there, was confronted on October 25, 1838, by a mob that lay in wait. Unhesitatingly, David Patton, whom Smith had named Captain Fearnot, ordered a charge. With the cry "God and Liberty," the Mormons charged the mob and put it to flight. A fleeing Missourian, hiding behind a tree, shot and killed the Mormon commander, and the Mormons, left without a leader, began to retreat.

On a late October afternoon in 1838, a mounted, hostile gentile mob appeared at Haun's Mill on the banks of Shoal Creek. Greatly outnumbered, many of the Mormons took refuge in the blacksmith's shop. A few even tried to negotiate with the invaders. The latter, however, opened fire on anyone in sight and, by poking their guns through the crevices in the log wall, killed fifteen men and women and two little boys, one of whom was hiding behind a bellows in the blacksmith's shop.

While confined in the crowded Liberty Jail with his fellow hostages, Joseph Smith kept up a constant correspondence with his followers and with his wife Emma and outlined his plans for the future in Zion. He thought with satisfaction about the Mormon temple planned for Far West, Missouri (the cornerstone had been laid in April 1838); but his mind was deeply concerned about the welfare of his people and a place for their permanent settlement.

During the defense of Far West, Missouri, Joseph Smith and other Church heads were invited to meet with mob leaders to work out a settlement of their difficulties. Upon their arrival at the meeting place, Joseph and his brethren were betrayed by one of his followers into the hands of the militia. After a mock trial before a court hastily convened on the spot by their persecutors, Joseph Smith and five of his companions were confined in the Liberty Jail where they were held for six months.

When Joseph and the other hostages were released from Liberty Jail in mid-April 1839, the governor's orders made it clear that the Mormons were not welcome. So again Joseph's people loaded their possessions into wagons and followed the Mississippi northward to the sparsely settled town of Commerce, Illinois. Joseph changed its name to Nauvoo, a Hebrew name signifying "a beautiful place," and began to organize a new city.

In the course of the Mormon wanderings, Joseph Smith preached to the Indians, who were known to the Mormons as Lamanites. He taught them that the Book of Mormon (he holds a copy of it in his hand) was the history of their people. Many Indians were deeply impressed by his message. Behind Joseph stands his brother Hyrum. The Mormon people have always taken a great interest in the welfare of the Indians.

Arrested on a charge of treason in June 1844, Joseph, his brother Hyrum, and two fellow Mormons were confined in the second story of a jail in Carthage, Illinois, to await trial. Promises had been given that the Carthage Grays, a local militia company, would protect the prisoners. Instead, they turned against the men, stormed the jail, and, despite a spirited defense, murdered Joseph and his brother. The killings occurred on the afternoon of June 27, and messengers were sent to spread the news.

Settled in Nauvoo, Joseph Smith, realizing that persecutions were inevitable, petitioned the state of Illinois for the right to organize a military body for protection of the Mormon community. The Nauvoo Legion, numbering about two thousand men (who carried on military training outside of their work and church duties), became one of the nation's largest militia. Here Joseph is reviewing the legion in full regalia.

When Joseph was hit by gunfire, his body fell through an upper window of the jail and landed beside the wellhouse in the yard below. Several more shots were fired into his body. Expecting reprisals, the assassins scattered, and citizens in the towns surrounding Carthage also feared revengeful moves by the Mormons. Born December 23, 1805, in Sharon, Vermont, Joseph Smith was thirty-eight years old at the time of his death.

The Nauvoo Temple was almost completed at the time Joseph Smith was murdered. It stood on the crest of the highest bluff in the center of the city, and the gleaming angel at the top of the spire could be seen for miles across the Illinois countryside. In 1844, the year of the Prophet's death, Nauvoo was said to have twenty thousand inhabitants, a population larger than Chicago's at that time. The Mormons' homes, businesses, and farms contributed to the city's prosperity.

Disheartened, the people planned to move from Nauvoo in the spring, but persecutions became so violent that their first wagon train for the almost unknown West crossed the Mississippi River on February 4, 1846. By February 15, the weather had become so bitterly cold that the wagon train was able to cross safely on the ice. At Sugar Creek, nine miles into Iowa and almost in view of their former homes in Nauvoo, a temporary camp was set up.

On the night of October 9, 1848, a Mormon-hating arsonist raced in darkness through the upper floors of the Nauvoo Temple. About three o'clock in the morning of October 10, flames burst suddenly from the tall spire, enveloping the gleaming angel, and those Mormons who were still in the vicinity saw their temple burn to the ground. Flames leaping high into the clear October sky were visible from great distances.

The force left behind by the Mormons to protect Nauvoo knew full well that the city could not be held for more than a few days, despite the strength and courage of the defenders. A gentile mob, preparing for an attack, surrounded a detachment of thirty Mormons under the command of Captain William Anderson, who was killed at the first volley.

The last Mormons driven from Nauvoo included many aged and ailing. At their first camp, near the Mississippi, they realized how poorly equipped they were for the westward trail. As they prepared their meager supper, they heard overhead a wild whirl of wings. Thousands of quail descended among them. Soon they had caught enough to insure their having wholesome food for the first few days of their journey.

The Mormon camp was crossing the Nebraska plains along the Platte River. They were so near their goal that detachments were sent out to find fertile ground in which to plant potatoes, buckwheat, and turnips. Said Brother Brigham Young humorously, "Prosecute the route as you have hitherto done until you arrive at some point in the Basin where you could hear the potatoes grow, if they had only happened to be there."

Driven from their homes in Nauvoo, the Mormons set out for the Rocky Mountains but, reaching the banks of the Missouri River, decided to make a temporary camp — a city of log cabins that they called Winter Quarters. This was the last settlement of any duration before the long trip across the plains. Around the brow of the nearby hill some six hundred were laid to rest; to this day the location is spoken of as the Mormon Boneyard.

On the last day of the long trek, President Young, weakened by mountain fever, mustered enough strength to ask Wilford Woodruff — in whose carriage he was riding — to turn the vehicle so that he might look out over the valley. From his seat the weary leader could see across the long sea of grass over which a misshapen cedar tree lifted its crooked limbs. "This is the place," he said.

(Captions for the Mormon Panorama series have been adapted from the original script by C.C.A. Christensen.)

MORMON POETRY ON THE THRESHOLD

Mormon poetry stands with Mormon poets — on the threshold . . . the poet can look back into the cool shadows 150 years long . . . look back into the Evangelistic joys of people who rode acrest of the American dream into the west of Manifest Destiny. Standing on that threshold, the Mormon poet can look into the brightness of day and see a light distorted by the shadows behind him. . . . The Mormon poet can look both ways but he can also look increasingly at the threshold itself and at himself standing with reluctant feet on that threshold . . . a product of the shadows and a shaper of the future. Standing there he can assess himself and what his Mormonness means to him.[1]

As man seeks for greater understanding of his role in life and his relationship to God and his fellowman, he also achieves an ever-greater capacity to express his comprehension of eternal truths.

Creativity, a virtue of the intellect, is an integral part of the glory of God. Something grand, a way of imitating God, and any great or even good poem carries like all the creations of God, the crest of the artist, and thus becomes the offspring of a mortal's immortal soul. In this sense poetry allows a mortal in embracing God's own images to fulfill his creation in God's own image.[2]

The Mormon poet, consciously or subconsciously, must inevitably draw from his understanding of Mormon philosophy when he pens his verse. As he depicts the scenes of life, he infallibly will infuse precepts and concepts of the Mormon faith. He will express Mormon values as he touches on whatever subject he treats. Thus, the Mormon poet has within his grasp a tremendous power: to blend the truths of the universe within the framework of the concise, beautiful, art of poetry.

ALLEN CORNWALL, *Editor*

---

[1]Richard Cracroft, from paper presented at the symposium: *On The Threshold.*
[2]*Ibid.*

MOUNTAIN MISTS — I have been interested in probing the spiritual or transcendental in my paintings. Perhaps I have been working in vain to project the spiritual through clumsy physical tools. Only time will tell to what extent I have succeeded.

WESLEY M. BURNSIDE, *Artist*

THE WORLD, IT SEEMS, IS STRANGELY CLEFT IN TWO

The world, it seems, is strangely cleft in two
As I stand all uncertain on this hill
And look upon thick foliage drenched with dew,
And rich black earth, and hear the whippoorwill
Sing sad songs which tear the heart
And make me think that this green world is still
Just misty prelude to a better part.
Such thoughts and hopes, though often too remote
To keep before me this life's counterpart,
Impel my heart at times toward that note
Sung to my soul from Eden's distant gate
And prompt me to unloose my willing throat
In praise of God at such a steady rate
That while I sing I seem to feel the hand
Of this world's savior, mankind's advocate,
Clasp round me softly like a golden band
And pull me nearer to my promised land.

JOHN B. HARRIS

THE PRUNING

It was time
To prune the apricots.
"Only one bud
Every few inches of tree
Or they won't grow,"
Said my father.

I didn't believe him,
Though,
And I kept one branch
All full of flowers,
For I knew
That come fall
They would all
Be beautiful and bright
And big--
Ever so big.

Early one moring
In fruit time
I ran to the orchard,
And beneath
The heavy-hanging
Golden crop
I harvested my apricots,
My many, many,
Tiny apricots.

When it was dark
I fed them
To the cow.

I prune now.

CAROL LYNN PEARSON

FLOYD E. BREINHOLT, *Artist*

TO THE GRAND TETON

I have seen your head in purple storm,
Serene, unpierced by lightning's rapier twist,
Impervious to thunderbolt, your form
Ethereal or bold in moving mist,--
By day a monarch ruling jewel-crowned,
Lake-mirrored granite gray and snow in blue,
A kingdom of contented sight and sound--
The legioned pines, the moose-cow in the slue.
No fear is on this land, yet at your feet,
Thin-covered by the earth's uncertain crust,
Unfathomed forces lie and spout their heat
In geysered vent and deep, infernal thrust.
And now, moon-bathed, your splendor glows with
    light
 In opal-fired and iridescent night.

On such a silver night as this a quake
Exploded Hebgen's summer-shadowed floor
And slid a mountain's tonnage, tipped a lake
And stopped a river — stilled forevermore
The laughter in the trees, the soft guitar,
The scurryings where dust alone was breath,
And here in testament a livid scar
And fissured earth remain — and death.
The cruel scarp along the mountain's length,
The drowning trees, the shore, betray the fault
Which undermined the valley's rock-ribbed strength--
When all seemed peace — in ruinous assault.
And where are they who trusted in its calm,
Nor read the printed warning in its palm?

If, suddenly, the force which gave you birth
Erupts its epicenter at your base,

Withstand the throes of inner-tortured earth,
Meet threat with strength along your granite face,
Travail with triumph. Ride the heaving crest.
Let avalanche but serve to shore your beams,
Survive as elk survive the antlered test,
Let molten rock be solder for your seams.
For you are symboled part of balanced law--
No stature unassailed is proven might--
Point and counterpoint; perfection, flaw.
If still you stand as now in noble height
When winds have swept the dark, volcanic cloud,
I shall be full of joy. I shall be proud!

ALICE MORREY BAILEY

51

THE ORDER IS LOVE

The Order Is Love is a musical play by Carol Lynn Pearson and Lex deAzevedo about the United Order. It was first produced by the College as the opening production of the Third Annual Mormon Festival of Arts. It was conceived and written over a number of years. When Carol Lynn Pearson did some reading about the United Order while in college, the subject struck her immediately as one that carried dramatic possibilities. She did some research, then tucked the idea away for that elusive "sometime" that many writers wait for.

Two years later she had the experience of living in a situation as close to the United Order, perhaps, as one can get today. She lived for three months on a kibbutz in Israel, where 600 people worked and ate together, each sharing quite equally in the responsibilities and the rewards of communal living. There, while picking oranges and weeding the cucumbers, Mrs. Pearson was again struck with the dramatic possibilities of life in the United Order.

Still, it was not until a few years, a husband, and one child later that Mrs. Pearson got to the actual writing of the play. The three of them spent the summer of 1969 in England and Scotland. For seven weeks they hid away on a small island in the Hebrides, Tiree, represented to them as "the sun spot of Great Britain." After three days of sunshine, the storms commenced and continued for the remainder of their stay. The temperature was about fifty-six, and the only sensible thing to do was to stay indoors by the electric fire and do what they had planned to do anyway — write.

It was during this time that *The Order Is Love* happened. Free from telephones and all outside obligations, Mrs. Pearson carefully reviewed her past research, outlined the play, and went to work. She corresponded with the foremost expert on the United Order, historian Leonard Arrington of Logan, Utah, to make certain that everything that went into the play was historically authentic. Four hours of writing per day for three weeks produced the original draft of *The Order Is Love*.

Returning to Utah, Mrs. Pearson approached Dean Lorin F. Wheelwright with the proposal that the play be done the following year as a part of the Mormon Festival of Arts. The dean and others responsible became interested in the work, and production wheels were set in motion.

About this time, Mrs. Pearson became acquainted with Lex deAzevedo, a returned missionary who was making an impressive reputation in California as a composer and musical director for motion pictures and for such TV productions as "The King Family Show" and "A Robert Young Special." Mr. deAzevedo agreed to write the musical score.

Selections from *The Order is Love* appear on Mormon Arts Recording I included with this volume.

Photo by WALLACE M. BARRUS

Of the play, historian Leonard J. Arrington wrote:

Records left by the more than one hundred United Orders suggest that the members were occasionally transported by transcendental experiences; they also suggest that there were occasional outcroppings of selfishness, arbitrariness, and maliciousness. Such aberrances were overcome by outpourings of good humor and good will. The pioneer Mormon capacity to pardon human imperfection and make the most of little opportunities and pleasures is captured by Carol Lynn Pearson in her happy musical *The Order Is Love.* Here is depicted the history and spirit of the Mormon pioneers. The meaning of the pioneer heritage — the selflessness, dedication, and enjoyment of life — is given authentic and imaginative expression in *The Order Is Love.* (From the foreword to the play.)

THE STORY

Ezra, one of the leaders of the order, introduces us to life in Orderville — 700 people living together, everybody equal, sharing the good and the bad, trying with their whole hearts to live the greatest of all commandments — love!

Two newcomers, Catherine Ann and her father, Brother Russell, arrive to join the order. Catherine Ann disdains life in Orderville. She wants to be an individual and live like "regular folks." She confides in Matthew, Ezra's son, that she came only because of her ailing father. She makes fun of his pants, which he has outgrown. Matthew defends the order and the life of self-denial it requires.

Later, at a dance, Matthew appears wearing a bright pair of store-bought pants, which he ingeniously obtained by shearing the wool off the discarded lambs' tails and trading it for pants. Catherine Ann is thrilled by this act, but the order's leaders reprimand Matthew for disobeying the rules.

Catherine Ann tries to adjust to the policies of Orderville, but after several failures she decides to go to Salt Lake City to live, leaving her father in Orderville. Life there goes on without her, but in time the order falters. Too many use it as a way to shirk responsibility; too many are discontent with the rules of the order. Some of the young people are attracted to the outside world.

Ezra pleads with the Board of Management not to make certain changes in the running of the order — ceasing of communal eating, bringing in a money system, and giving different compensations for different types of labor. But the members want the changes, which are then agreed upon by common consent.

Catherine Ann, learning of her father's death, returns to Orderville, finds Matthew, and concludes that all that really counts in life is the people that you love. The play ends on the note that the order is not really finished — that someday, someway, man's dream of brotherhood will come true — if everyone just keeps learning a little more about love.

WALLACE M. BARRUS, *Photographer*

This song, "A Little More Love," describes what the world could be if everyone would really live like brothers:

I see a world where every man's a brother,
I see a world where every man will share.
I see a world where not one soul
Is left alone or cold,
A world where every man
Is loved, and clothed and fed.

I see a world that's heaven here around us,
Where we can
Practice up for paradise.
It isn't far away--
We'd be there in a day,
If every man in every land would pay the price.

A little more love
Will make it happen.
A little more love
Will make it come true.
A little more love
Will make it happen.
A little less me,
And a little more you

The field you sow with love grows gold as sunrise,
The house you build from love is filled with light.
To do for someone else
Instead of just yourself
Like magic makes a dark world bright.

The man from Galilee said "Love thy neighbor,"
Then hate and war and sorrow all will die.
The way he came to teach
Is right within our reach
If every man in every land would only try.

A little more love
Will make it happen.
A little more love
Will make it come true.
A little more love
Will make it happen.
A little less me,
A little more you.
And a little more you.
A little more love.

The pain of growing up is poignantly described by Catherine Ann as she sings "The Weeping Willow":

So long ago I used to muse
Within a childish wonder deep,
And ask myself with great concern
Do weeping willows really weep?

And when I went to school to learn
The things one learns to make one wise.
I thought, How foolish, trees don't weep,
For weeping things have tearful eyes.

But now that I have tasted more
Of learning than the wise men taught,
I sit again beneath my tree
With wisdom much more dearly bought.

My eyes are pale, blue-desert dry,
As with the swaying leaves I sigh:
Oh, foolish they who cannot see
The weeping of the willow tree--

The weeping of the tree--
And me.

LAEL J. WOODBURY, *Editor*

(See recording for these and other selections.)

55

W-2 FORM

"The elements are the tabernacle of God." (D&C 93:35.) These words inspired an experiment in the theatre entitled *W-2 Form*, which was presented at Brigham Young University in March, 1970, under this author's conception and direction. The production was a conscious attempt to demonstrate the validity of that scripture and to explore a similar statement made by the master architect Mies van der Rohe: "God is in the details."

Noting that music, the most abstract of the arts, is the form having the highest status and frequency of production in the Church, the author decided to orchestrate additional abstract elements for artistic purposes. As the musician structures sound elements, perhaps he might structure light, color, rhythm, movement, time, taste, texture, temperature, and language.

to discover and present elements of the macro — and micro world — elements that most conclusively demonstrate God's presence and influence.

The theatre is especially adept at depicting elements and details. With today's advanced technology of sound, light, and film, it is possible to display the symmetry and the beauty of a microscopic cell as a metaphor for the symmetry and beauty of God. With it we can suggest the fact and quality of God in the order, complexity, and form of abstract sound; in the architectural detail of a beloved building; in the resonance of color, texture, rhythm; in the variety and beauty of human form and movement; in sculpture, light, glass, paper; possibly in the infinite moods of a human kiss; or in that electrifying moment when the force of God's revelation churns through the flesh of man.

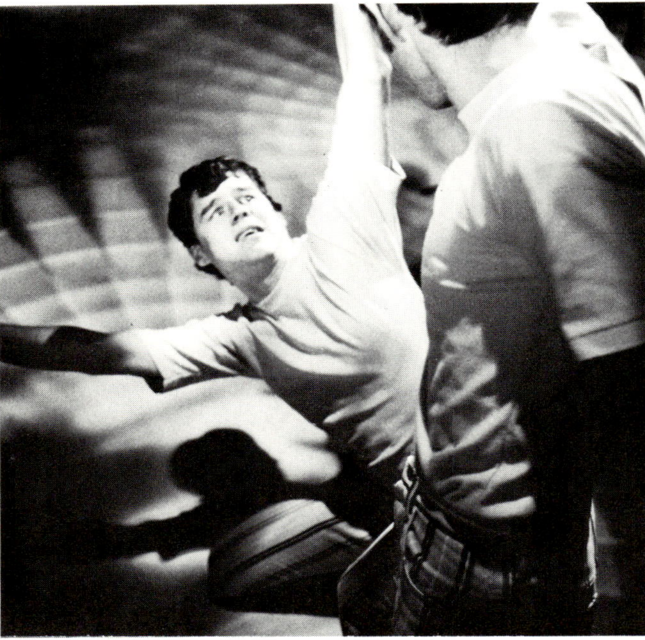

In what form? There is no compelling reason why a theatre work must have a beginning, a middle, and an end. It need not exhibit actors, tell a story, or even use language. It might follow the example of poetry, which presents a series of images in juxtaposition. We might create a theatrical poetry by presenting visual or aural or other sense images that generate new perceptions as conventional poetry does.

And to what end? Surely such theatre pieces must entertain, but they might also analyze important ideas, values, and convictions. In this godless age, for example, the need for God is unparalleled. But where shall we find him? In service stations, factories, parking lots, swimming pools, or movie houses? It is difficult to find God in the everyday world.

But, according to the scripture again, "The elements are the tabernacle of God." With this insight, the company of *W-2 Form* determined

W-2 Form, then, was an attempt to express in theatrical terms a vision of God, a conviction that he lives, and that our world and universe accurately mirror him. It consisted of twenty-one episodes — such as voice collages relating four stories simultaneously, a silent movie, an examination of colored fabrics under intense and varied light, a plexiglass heroic sculpture of the human family, an examination of the qualities of the earth's flowers that move from cellular studies to photographs of exotic blooms displayed on three screens and the floor of the theatre, which served as a fourth screen. The production employed twelve projectors and 763 slides. It also presented dancers in white, who moved under intricate projected patterns. It concluded with an examination of the beauty and intricacy of the Salt Lake Temple's architecture.

The temple sequence began with rare photographs, supplied by the National Aeronautics and Space Administration, of the universe. Especially impressive were photographs of the earth shown in relation to other elements of the heavens. As we moved from galaxies to solar systems to planets, and eventually to the earth's atmosphere, we rested upon minute details of the temple. Then, for some time, we explored the beauty there — the sheen of a balustrade polished by the hands of multiple generations, the curve of a tiny carving, the texture of granite half in light and half in shadow, the temple's artful iron and copper work. After awhile, the cameras moved back and displayed sufficient perspective for the audience to discover, for the first time, that it had been viewing details of the temple. As the photos revealed more of the building, and the accompanying music became more expansive, the screens displayed again the morning and evening sun; clouds; the moon over the temple; stars; and eventually the macro world with which the sequence began.

The theme of the production is summarized in this fragment of a poem, by Dennis Smith, which was spoken in the performances:

> I climbed up here,
> (a place my brother made last year)
> between three cottonwoods.
>
> And I enjoy the majesty I feel
> when I come up
> and look out over orchard trees--
> so flat that all their tops
> look like a carpet
> and I feel like I could dance the air
> across it
> if I wanted.
> . . . .
> I may be
> awfully high
> here in my poplar tree.
> Still I wonder
> if there isn't someone
> higher up than I am
>
> in a taller poplar,
> looking down at me?

LAEL J. WOODBURY

W-2 FORM PICTURE SEQUENCE — In a voice and movement collage, two actors present the similar conflicts between Orpheus and Eurydice, Jacob and the Angel, and Brer Rabbit and the Tar Baby (left-opposite page). Light, color, and movement react differently upon a moving figure, white and colored fabric, flat and curved planes, hard and soft surfaces (center). Man is more than personality, he is form, even architecture. The endless complexity of the human form acquires additional meaning when studied under artful lighting, with special costumes, or when juxtaposed with contrasting lines, surfaces, and materials (right). The plexiglas sculpture (left above) by Trevor Southey, depicts the human family — parents and children — in three stages of its existence: pre-mortal, mortal and immortal. By viewing each dimension through the other two, as this sculpture permits, one sees their parts as a whole, and observes that the human family is a continuum, a truly eternal relationship. (See also p. 41.)

THE TRAGEDY OF KORIHOR

The Tragedy of Korihor, an original dramatization of a Book of Mormon character and situation, was presented at Brigham Young University on March 19, 1971, by BYU's Touring Repertory Theatre Company. For a year prior to that date, this play was presented by the company on tour through the Rocky Mountain states as well as in Texas, California, Oregon, and Washington. It was directed by Dr. Harold I. Hansen.

The play's author, Louise G. Hanson, began the play while enrolled in a playwriting class. There she was assigned to write a play about a reprehensible historical character and to treat him sympathetically. The purpose of the exercise was to develop the ability to depict well-developed characters — to discover and make clear even those motives that animate evil men.

Mrs. Hanson says:

The account of Korihor in the Book of Mormon being very brief, my problem was to make him a real person, someone with whom the audience could identify. Did he have a family? What was his vocation? If he had known God and Christ, what weakness in his character allowed Satan to overpower him until he denied the existence of Deity? How would his new satanic philosophy affect his family, the people to whom he preached, even himself?

Some of the answers to these questions can be found, of course, in the Book of Mormon account. Korihor's weakness in character was his resistance to the spirit of truth (Alma 30:46); his satanic philosophies set the Nephite people against each other, influencing them to perversity and wickedness (Alma 30:13-18), finally bringing about his own debilitating dumbness and ignominious death (Alma 30:50, 59). But I fabricated Korihor's profession, choosing to make him a lawyer because of the Book of Mormon account of his sophistical reasoning. And in order to strike a sympathetic chord in the hearts of playgoers, I conceived Korihor at the outset as a loving family man who had taught his son to love God and Christ, who had always treated his wife with affectionate deference, who felt tenderness toward his daughter-in-law and pride in his infant grandson. Gradually, then, I could show Korihor's weakness overcoming his spiritual strength, alienating his family from him one by one, causing his devoted wife to lose her mind from grief, leaving him with his followers who remained with him only as long as he could lead them to power and wealth but who abandoned him when his power was stripped from him.

Although my script for *Korihor* is not, therefore, verbatim from the Book of Mormon, the message of the Book of Mormon account of Korihor's tragedy is also the play's message: Man must "lean not to his own understanding" but must be obedient to the will, the spirit, and the commandments of God. It is a relevant message in today's world where people are turning more and more away from God, denying his existence, depending upon their own intellect which at its most sublime is far below God's.

LAEL J. WOODBURY, *Editor*

WALLACE M. BARRUS, *Photography*

THE APOSTATE

The Apostate is a new play based on the story of the rebellion and the eventual conversion of Alma the Younger. (See Mosiah 27.) Written in modern American idiom, the play attempts to portray the classic father-son relationship, with its full love-hate dimension, in a setting and language familiar to today's audiences.

The play was written by Orson Scott Card, directed by Dr. Charles W. Whitman, and presented for the first time on March 18, 1971, at Brigham Young University.

One of the most novel aspects of the production is its treatment of the ancient prophet. Instead of deifying Alma the Elder, and making him personally infallible, the playwright shows him as a man capable of error, needing to turn to the Lord for help. This approach, felt the playwright, makes Alma's divine calling all the more ennobling, since its exercise becomes a challenge, not just a privilege.

Concerning the purpose of the play, the author wrote:

If I am an artist, then I must be a Mormon artist; for the Mormon culture is irrevocably in me. My purpose in writing is not to proselyte, but rather to help the not-yet-sanctified Mormon on his way, and to provide the Latter-day Saint a venture into joy. Where better to do this than in theatre, where prophets and apostates can live again, where actors and directors living close to the spirit of the Lord can move audiences not only emotionally and intellectually, but also spiritually? If even for a moment my work can do this, then I have succeeded in the noblest purpose of any artist.

LAEL J. WOODBURY, *Editor*

WALLACE M. BARRUS, *Photographer*

59

MORMON VIGNETTES

The Mormon Festival of Arts introduced a new and promising mode of dramatic performance. Recognizing that intimate human experience is the most informative and interesting artistic substance, the festival featured an evening of dramatic, first-person narratives based on documented experiences.

Sometimes these short works were recited by actors in costume; sometimes they were read aloud; and other times they were presented in a more conventional fashion by a company of actors. Based on diaries, family traditions, and personal knowledge, these insights into human problems and decisions reaffirm that man's relationships with his environment and with other men — or women — evidently persist because they are part of the divine plan.

These two Mormon vignettes are typical of those presented.

LAEL J. WOODBURY

WALLACE M. BARRUS, *Photographer*

THE HEALING

(A reading of excerpts from *The Healing* appears on Mormon Arts Recording I, included with this volume.)

Sarah stares into the sterile land and no longer smiles or weeps. The tears last came when a band of rebel Indians burned our wagon and our child. That was a prairie and a mountain range ago, a dozen snowstorms since.

Before we headed west, we had a farm with fertile fields. Sarah walked beside me, behind the horse, and we dug deep furrows, planted seed wheat, and laughed and worked together. When the day was still high, we lay together and made a child. That was when times were fertile, when land yielded, and when Sarah's belly was full of promise.

I praised God then. I embraced the news that God had raised a prophet in the latter days. When the Prophet said, "Move west," I gave up my fields and home, and loaded the wagon bed with wheat, enough wheat to make a golden path from east to west. We travelled from the land of promise to the promised land — my wife, my child, and bursting bags of wheat. But God saw the wasteland and stayed behind in the fertile valleys. There is no God here.

This land is harsh. It holds no promise. Only one tree in this wilderness dares defy the earth-rock existence, the unrelenting wind, and the waist-high snow mounds. Only a tree and a man defy the elements. A man with a woman-shell, a horse, and a single bag of seed wheat. The horse brought us this far, but when the spring comes, it will return us to our land from whence we came. We must find again a living God, a place where wheat and another child will grow.

When the snows fell, we burrowed like moles into the hillside and made a shelter. Roots hang cobweblike and brush our faces. Occasionally a snake drops down upon us, but Sarah doesn't scream. Her eyes are covered with wagon smoke.

I turn my back to the shelter and survey the land but see only the white glaze of snow and the lone cottonwood. Is the cottonwood strong because it has battled the elements and won, or is it strong in spite of the rocky soil? Can a man become strong in these craggy hills? Can he master the land and bend with the wind? Or does he break as shale and peel back layer by layer until there is nothing left?

The horse whinnies, a friendly sound . . . the horse, my link with survival. With my horse I can again furrow fertile fields and make seed children grow. Here? Would wheat grow here? The ground is hard baked from summer sun and centuries of buffalo and wild horse hoofs. What lies beneath the stone and clay-baked earth?

Again the horse whinnies. I see moving figures silhouetted on the horizon. I quickly go inside and move Sarah further into the shadows. Her body, once full and warm, is light and has no substance. She offers no resistance.

I hear hoofbeats and go to meet whatever comes.

The granite cliffs mirror the faces of five Indians who stand before me. Their stone faces are etched with ice. Their eyes avoid looking at the horse or Sarah, and yet they see them both. They stare at me, calculating, cold; and I stare back, defying all.

The horse whinnies, and before they speak, I know what they want.

"Horse." their voices demand.

"No." I know I gamble. They could take the horse and kill me in a single gesture. Their faces never seem to move, even when they speak.

"Horse." Indians are cold like the country they inhabit.

"No horse."

From within his clothes the leader takes a child, a tiny Indian child, and swings it by the feet.

"Indian for horse." He wants to trade! They have no feelings. They can barter a child for an animal. It's probably a stolen child.

"No horse."

He walks toward the cottonwood and swings the child. He is going to kill it! He takes one swing and narrowly misses slamming the child's head against the broad-trunked tree. It is no idle threat. He means to bash its head against the tree! What he doesn't know is that I hate Indians, old and young. One child, one Indian child, more or less, will not make me give up my only chance for survival.

The wind whistles around me, cutting through me. But stronger than the wind blows all the hate I have for this godless land, for the lost happiness of love, even for my belief that made me give up everything, and especially for the men who burn children.

"Indian or horse."

Damn it, stop swinging that child like a squealing rabbit.

"No horse."

The Indian swings the child back—a child who still gives no cry. I see its eyes now watering from the stinging wind.

"Stop."

It is my voice that cries out.

"Take the horse."

The Indian drops the child into the snow and takes my horse who whinnies and is gone.

Again the land is still. The wind whips snow against my legs and I hate the cottonwood for resisting. I move over to the child and look upon it. Its skin is the color of the summer earth, and the blackness of its eyes leave little space for white. I pick up the child and hold it an arm length from me. What can I do with a woman-shell, a single sack of seed wheat, and an Indian child? I move toward the shelter. I bring the child toward me to gain better balance and feel the child's warmth.

An Indian, warm!

I walk into the dug-out hill and place the child in Sarah's arms. The baby turns its head and searches for food.

Sarah bows her head and sees the child. Her arms feel its warmth. She pulls it close and raises her eyes to me.

"Oh God, Sarah! Tears!"

JANICE DIXON

[1]Author's note: My great-grandfather, Stephen Markham, saved a Piute Indian child from a band of Ute Indians. They named the child Julia and raised her with their own family. You might say that she was the first in the Indian Placement Program. Julia grew to adulthood and married a Mexican boy named Juan. She returned several times to my grandfather's home to show her own family. The manner in which she was saved is factually presented in my vignette.

THE MISSIONARY

You know, Louis, this is the happiest day of my life! It's hard for me to believe that you are really here beside me. I know everyone always thinks of his wedding as the most unique and important happening on the face of God's good earth, but . . . well, we *do* seem to share a specialness that others lack.

It's easy for me to remember the first time I saw you. I was eighteen and newly baptized. Fresh from the mission home, you arrived at our place looking terribly bewildered and *very* dusty from that long train ride. When I answered the door, you looked like you were going to bolt; you were so sure you'd gone to the wrong house! I can still see Mama bustling around—preparing your room, trying to introduce you to the other elder, keeping the younger children from nosing in your suitcase, and asking a running stream of questions about yourself on the side!

Mama was always so happy when a new elder came. It was really hard for her to live in the mission field in Bozeman, so far away from Norway. Dad never was a religious man although he felt the Church had much to offer him. I remember how hard you tried to convince him to sell the brewery and join. Isn't it funny that only the women in my family actually joined the Church?

Grandma heard the gospel in Oslo and followed the Church to Salt Lake with Mama in tow. That's where Mama and Dad met—right here. They stood over there in the late afternoon sun, trying to ask directions of someone who didn't know a word of Norwegian and getting more frustrated by the minute. Dad had been here awhile, working his way back and forth across the country, and had a pretty good command of English as well as his native Norwegian.

I like to think it was love at first sight for them.

At any rate, they got married two months later and moved to Montana. Mama worked with the few other members there to organize a branch, with our home as the center.

Mama said Dad didn't want to join because he wouldn't be able to argue about something with her anymore, but he was always home for evening prayer and saw that we children were always in church on Sunday.

Dad sure liked you. He always said to me, "Anna, that young man is different. Seems to know what he wants from life." And then he would add with a sly smile, "He'd make a mighty fine husband!" Secretly, I agreed with him. But it was hard to lay traps. You were dedicated to your call, and I didn't feel it was my place to distract you. Also you told us all about your sweetheart back home who was waiting for you. That kind of hurt my pride; you would praise her looks and then tease me about being so skinny that I'd disappear if I turned sideways! But we did talk, and I was always impressed with your sensitivity to people and things around you. You seemed to know how people felt and what they were thinking. No wonder our membership grew so fast while you were there.

I really idolized you.

Then it came time for you to leave, and I hid in my room because I didn't want to say goodbye. Mama and Dad called and called for me, but you *knew* where I was. When I heard the soft knock on my door and your voice gently saying, "Anna," I couldn't hold back the tears anymore. You then told me how you felt about me—that I was a special person for you but it was the wrong time and that the Lord would bring us back together when it was the *right* time. I didn't really believe you—then. But I waited twelve years before I married another, always hoping you'd come back for me. Whenever we got a letter from you (not as often as I would have liked!), the family would all sit and read it together. You told us about your job teaching school, your advancement in your Church positions, and . . . your growing family. I'd always been a dreamer, and I had *hundreds* of dreams, all ending with me as your wife.

Finally, I met George and I married him. I was tired of being lonely, and he was extremely handsome and outgoing. Now I had children to write about! Our families grew up and we lost contact with each other.

Then one day I got that letter from you, and I could hardly believe my eyes! My husband had been dead for many years, and your wife had died the year before. You told me such a strange story. You had been asleep when my father had appeared before you with such a sad, beseeching look on his face that you woke up and felt compelled to find me. You thought some genealogy had been left undone. Well, in a way it had. I wasn't sealed to anyone yet!

You found me and we corresponded for a while; then you came and visited me for two weeks. I knew you were going to propose and kept wondering why it took you so long!

They say that the best years of our lives are when we are young, but we are in our seventies and have found a happiness in our love for each other and the Lord that many younger people never find. I love you, Louis, now and forever.

ANNE GRAFF

WALLACE M. BARRUS, Photographer

THE KIRTLAND TEMPLE

A Mormon temple is a house of the Lord — an awesome distinction.

The one at Kirtland, Ohio, is exceptional. The sacrifices required to build it, the glorious events attending its dedication, the keys restored therein, and the worldwide consequences that followed have no counterpart in history.[1]

In December of 1830, only eight months after the organization of the Church, came the command to gather at Ohio. A further command was given on December 27, 1832:

It is my will that you should build a house. If you keep my commandments, you shall have power to build it.

If you keep not my commandments, the love of the Father shall not continue with you, therefore you shall walk in darkness.[2]

The Saints were poor and less than two thousand in number. But the Lord did not consider their poverty an excuse. On June 1, 1833, another command, which included a rebuke, was given the Saints, instructing them to proceed at once.

To begin a structure that was to cost $70,000 was an optimistic undertaking, indeed, and attests to the Saints' belief in the promise of the Lord: "If you keep my commandments you shall have power to build it."[3]

. . . the sisters went to work and made stockings, pantaloons, and jackets. . . . Our wives were all the time knitting, spinning, and sewing, and in fact, I may say doing all kinds of work; they were just as busy as any of us.[4]

62

On June 6, 1833, a conference of high priests assembled and instructed the building committee to immediately obtain stone, brick, lumber, and other materials. On July 23 the cornerstones of the Lord's house were laid, after the order of the holy priesthood.

However, bitter opposition surged about the Saints. They sometimes posted armed guards, and bodyguards slept near the Prophet to give the alarm should he be attacked. Despite the scarcity of currency and the problems with the mobs, however, the Saints of Kirtland continued

their work, for the remembrance of the Lord's promise gave them faith to continue.

Joseph Smith, the president of the Church, acted as foreman of the stone quarry; Hyrum Smith helped dig the foundation trenches. Hour after hour, sweating horses toiled up the hill, dragging huge blocks of limestone for the foundation and walls. Strong-armed men hoisted the stones into position, and masons fixed them firmly with cement. Every male member was expected to give one-seventh of his time to the building without pay. Those who worked on it at day's wages had no other income; wages were paid in cornmeal.

In order to get enough officers to lay the cornerstones in Kirtland, the Saints had to ordain boys fifteen and sixteen years of age as elders.

When the Lord commanded his people to build a house, he gave them the pattern by vision from heaven; the size of the house, the form of the pulpits, and everything pertaining to it were clearly pointed out by revelation. God gave a vision of these things not only to Joseph Smith but also to several others.

The lower auditorium is decorated with beautifully carved columns and arches. Adding to the simple beauty are the elevated pulpits, situated in the east and west ends of the auditorium. These represent the two priesthoods found in Christ's church. The initials embossed in gold on each section designate some of the ministerial officers.

The center and sides are constructed to allow worship toward either end of the building; that is, within each pew there is a movable bench that allows the congregation to face the pulpits nearest them. The pews are sectioned or "fenced" by low railings, and one enters each section through a low, swinging door that can be locked. With this seating plan a method of "sectional division" was used, permitting the division of the auditorium into two or four sections by curtains. These white curtains were dropped from the ceilings by ropes that passed through small holes. They could be lowered or raised as desired. Narrow spaces between the pews allowed them to reach the floor.

One of the supporting columns housed a dumbwaiter device, which brought up and lowered the sacramental bread and wine.

Entering the classrooms on the third floor, one gets the feeling of stepping into a nineteenth-century school; there are roughly laid floorboards, small windows, and low ceilings. Here the priesthood attended specific instructional classes.

Finally the glorious day of dedication arrived. Then all labors ceased: hammers, saws, and paintbrushes were laid aside. Work clothes were exchanged for Sunday's best. The Saints relaxed and looked over the work of art. It was Sunday, March 27, 1836. That day heralded the most glorious of all the spiritual blessings of the Kirtland period. That day began a period of true pentecost, as chosen ones were endowed with power from on high.

Great throngs assembled, and a multitude were unable to obtain admittance to the services. By nine o'clock in the morning, seats and aisles were jammed with men, women, and children who had spent long hours in the construction work. Many were turned away at the door because there was no room for them inside, even though children sat on the laps of their parents.

Those from all the nearby branches of the Church, and even a few from Missouri, journeyed to Kirtland afoot, on horses, or in wagons to witness the event. Donations amounting to $963 were contributed at the doors.

The Prophet Joseph and Presidents Rigdon and Cowdery seated the congregation as they came in and, according to their calculation, received between nine and ten hundred — as many as could be comfortably seated. The meeting began with the song "Now Let Us Rejoice," and President Joseph Smith gave the beautiful dedicatory prayer.

The journals of many who attended the service record that angels appeared in the congregation and that heavenly choirs sang. Many were aware of a divine presence that filled the temple, for they had kept the commandments of God, and the love of the Father continued with them.

During the dedicatory ceremonies, an angel appeared and sat near Joseph Smith, Sr., and Frederick G. Williams so that they had a fair view of his person. He was tall and had black eyes, white hair, and stooped shoulders. His garment was whole, extending to near his ankles; on his feet he had sandals. He was sent as a messenger to accept the dedication.

At one point the choir, stationed in the four corners of the temple, together with the assembly fervently sang "The Spirit of God Like a Fire Is Burning." For the glory of the Lord had filled the house of God. Then followed the hosanna shout of adoration: "Hosanna, Hosanna to God and the Lamb, amen, amen, and amen." It was repeated three times. This shout was used when the Saints entered the Salt Lake Valley in 1847 and has been used at all temple dedications since that time.

An event of the greatest significance occurred on April 3, 1836, after a Sabbath day meeting. It was recorded by the Prophet himself.

I retired to the pulpit, the veils being dropped, and bowed myself, with Oliver Cowdery, in solemn and silent prayer, the following vision was opened to both of us: The Veil was taken from our minds, and the eyes of our understanding were opened. We saw the Lord standing upon the breastwork of the pulpit before us, and under his feet was a paved work of pure gold in color like amber. His eyes were as a flame of fire, the hair of his head was white like the pure snow, his countenance shone above the brightness of the sun, and his voice was as the sound of great waters.

After this vision closed, the heavens were again opened unto us and Moses appeared before us, and committed unto us the keys of the gathering of Israel from the four parts of the earth, and the leading of the Ten Tribes from the land of the north. After this Elias appeared, and committed the dispensation of the Gospel of Abraham, saying, that in us, and in our seed, all generations after us should be blessed. After this vision had closed, another great and glorious vision burst upon us, for Elijah the Prophet, who was taken to heaven without tasting death, stood before us."[5]

One evening the Prophet met with the quorums in the temple. Brother George A. Smith stood up and began to prophesy. Suddenly a noise like the sound of mighty rushing wind filled the building. A brilliant pillar of light rose above the structure. All the congregation arose, in an instant, being moved upon by an invisible power. Many began to speak in tongues and prophesy; others saw glorious visions. The temple was filled with angels. People from the neighborhood came running toward the temple, having heard the unusual sound and seen the brilliant light. Thus, not only the Saints were aware of these manifestations of the Spirit but people of the community as well.

The dedication of the Kirtland Temple was a glorious time for the Latter-day Saints. They had built a house of prayer, of fasting, of faith, of learning, of glory, of order — a house of God. They had kept the commandments of their Father, and they continued in his love.

However, human nature being what it is, the Saints' adversaries viewed the temple, and those who built it, as something worthy of destruction; persecution increased manyfold. Mutiny broke out in the rank and file of Church membership. Apostasy reached a climax in the latter months of 1837, when over half of the Kirtland membership either left the Church or were excommunicated.

As the Saints drank in the spirit of the world, the Spirit of the Lord withdrew from their hearts. Priesthood meetings in the temple threatened several times to break into armed fights, and swords were worn in the temple meetings. Many acts of violence followed in close sequence. Brigham Young stated:

The Temple at Kirtland had fallen into the hands of wicked men, and by them polluted, like the temple at Jerusalem, and consequently disowned by the Father and the Son.[6]

Therefore, the Saints were driven from Kirtland, and what was once a place of glory now became a barn!

The Kirtland Temple represents a historical paradox. What was once a temple of God, in which the Lord Jesus Christ appeared personally, became but a house — a building whose sole claim to distinction lay in its wondrous past. It is today a living reminder that an impossible goal can be won through righteousness and faith in God and that the consequences of disobeying eternal commandments are inescapable.

A Graduate Project
under the Supervision of
Dr. Lael J. Woodbury

---

[1]See Clarence L. Fields, "History of the Kirtland Temple," unpublished Master of Science thesis (Brigham Young University, 1963) for a more detailed account of this building, its history, and its purposes.
[2]D&C 05:11-12.
[3]D&C 95:3.
[4]Heber C. Kimball, *Journal of Discourses*, (Los Angeles: Gartner Printing and Litho Co., Inc., 1956), X, 165.
[5]DHC, I, 435-436; D&C 110.
[6]Cecil McGavin, "The Kirtland Temple Defiled," *Improvement Era*, XLIII (October 1940), 594.

KENNETH L. BEVAN, *Photographer*

CREATIVE DRAMATICS

Creative dramatics attempts to make every child a participant instead of a spectator, a doer instead of a watcher. In traditional theater, the audience members are the most important element; in creative dramatics, however, the child is the center. Thus, one child, Tommy, might toss an imaginary ball to his classmate, who plays that he is Tommy's dog. "Go get it Spot!" calls Tommy, and Spot scampers after the ball as playfully as any real-life dog would. Then Tommy's mother steps outside and asks, "Tommy, would you go milk? I need some milk to make a cake." And Tommy and Spot go into the pasture to fetch the cows.

Children begin — under proper leadership — with simple, individual pantomimes. These are expanded to include group pantomimes, such as a trip to the beach, which require vivid imaginations. With this type of activity as a foundation, children then expand their creative powers by playing various roles that require characterizations unlike themselves.

The children learn to develop their own dramatic story. First, the basic story line is established. It must contain a beginning, a climax, and a satisfying ending. Then the children present the story, and it is followed by an evaluation session. Although the children's memory span is relatively short, each presentation improves as they seek answers to such questions as, "What did we like about the cow?" or "What was it that Mother said to Tommy that helped him make his part seem more real?"

This process calls for much leadership skill. The children must feel that their ideas are of worth and that the leader is not forcing his ideas upon them.

Dramatic play is natural for children. Creative dramatics, however, introduces several additional concepts beyond the free play of children. First, an adult leader must be present to focus and guide the attention and activities of the group. He helps the children to organize their ideas into workable relationships. The story idea may come from a retold story, given by the leader, or the children may choose to create their own story.

The value of this creative endeavor is manifold. Individually the children learn to think for themselves, using problem-solving techniques. They find self-expression and individual identity. Their emotions find healthy expression. Often, normally shy children begin to participate in nonspeaking roles. As they grow in self-confidence, they may accept speaking roles. No role is permanently assigned, but the children can volunteer for the various roles in each presentation. The leader sees that every child receives equal opportunity for performance.

In addition, participants learn to interact with one another in harmonious relationships. They learn to plan and cooperate with others for a desired effect. By role playing they come to understand the position of others. They also learn to seek new alternatives and new solutions to problems.

Society traditionally looks upon a person with disfavor whenever he exhibits signs of nonconformity — particularly in the classroom. The usual procedure is to try to teach children to conform, to follow the rules. But every person deserves the right and opportunity to become his own best self, to discover his own ways and means of expression. Intellectual achievement is not the only measure of his worth. Dr. Calvin Taylor has demonstrated very capably that a child may be rated a relatively low academic achiever but that this same child may excel in communicative or decision-making abilities. He feels that we need to recognize the multiple talents of people and nurture their creative tendencies.

Creative dramatics offers one way, an excellent way, of encouraging children to become more expressive, more innovative people.

LAEL J. WOODBURY, *Editor*

If thou art merry, praise the Lord with singing, with music, with dancing, and with a prayer of praise and thanksgiving.

D & C 136:28

THE SWEET SINGER OF ISRAEL

Let me be happy too. Oh! Restless soul,
  Fold thy quick limbs and rest from care a while;
Watch the great clouds in fleecy volumes roll;
  The lakelet in the sunshine seems to smile; --
Would God my friends were here to share my thought, --
  Would I could find the rest I long have sought.

Would I could speak the language of the hills
  Would their plush velvet grace I could make known;
Could I translate the talking of the rills
  That from their crowning dimples wander down, --
I would not sing, and yet I can not cease;
  I can not murmur, yet I have no peace.[1]

Thus wrote David Hyrum Smith in December 1870. He was the fifth son of the martyred prophet, the youngest brother of Joseph Smith III, and a missionary, counselor, artist, and poet. The poem is a song of discontent and so he labeled it. But perhaps more than that it is the effort of a simple and poetic man to make his voice heard.

David Hyrum Smith was born in Nauvoo on November 17, 1844, five months after the assassination of his father. The impact of this tragedy made its mark on the young man. Opportunities were few and David's education was limited, but he early indicated an almost unlimited interest in his environment. He was an avid reader and an artistically talented young man. Passionately fond of music, flowers, and people, his education was primarily self-created from these interests. When he was baptized into the Reorganization in October 1861, the Montrose, Iowa Branch was informed that David was to be "one of our church pillars, for the Spirit says so."[2]

United with his brothers in Nauvoo, he grew in stature and insight, taking on the physical characteristics of the Smiths and the attitudes of his older brother. He was ordained a priest in March 1863, and seven months later at Council Bluffs, Iowa, he was ordained an elder. Following this he was assigned to work in the Michigan and northern Indiana areas, traveling often with either Joseph or Alexander.[3]

The conference of 1869, meeting in Saint Louis, optimistically appointed David and his older brother, Alexander, to Utah and the Pacific Slope to contact the "scattered saints" there. The brothers returned from their not-too-successful mission in March 1870 — Alexander, because of his wife's illness, and David, "on account of being too incapacitated by illness for the field."[4]

Yet in May 1870, David was strong enough to marry eighteen-year-old Clara Charlotte Hartshorn at the home of her parents at Sandwich, deKalb, Illinois. Their son, Elbert Aorivl, was born at the Mansion House in Nauvoo in March of the following year.[5]

Soon after his return from Utah, David was called to the First Presidency of the Reorganization by a message on March 3, 1873, and was ordained at the conference.[6]

It was increasingly evident that David's health had weakened, for he suffered a "severe attack of brain fever." Less than a year after his ordination, the *Herald* reported that "Brother Smith is ill again." Then again in April, "David is at Nauvoo where he will probably remain during the summer and fall . . . he seems to be recuperating."[7]

Unfortunately, the illness did not decline during the resting period, and David became more and more of a problem to the community. An inquiry was held at Yorkville. With little or no hesitation, a commitment order was authorized, and David was committed to the Illinois Hospital for the Insane on January 10, 1877.

In the afternoon of August 29, 1904, David Hyrum Smith died. The cause of his death was directly related, it was said, to his illness — termed here as *melancholia dementia*.

A poet by nature as well as activity, there was early evidence that this sensitive member of a sensitive family felt the need to express some of the ideas and feelings that were being associated in his mind. Deeply moved by things beautiful, melancholy at times, yet strangely well tempered and overflowing with humor, love, sympathy, and humility, he felt compelled to speak what was often unspoken.

During his association at Nauvoo, he discovered a place, just back of the Mansion House by a waterfall, which formed a natural amphitheater overlooking the grassy slope and the water. There he would read and write and meditate — often spending long hours with his thoughts. This retreat, called "David's Chamber," was probably the inspiration for his best statement of his attachment to nature:

In every nook some sight of beauty wakes a tender thought;
  Some flower blooming by some old gray stone;
Or tiny bird's nest with abundant skill and labor wrought;
  Or faithful shadow over shining waters thrown.
  The thickets darkly dense and still,
  Where scarce the slender vine leaves thrill; --
  Unbend, oh brow! and sad heart, take thy fill
  Of rest, beside the lonely woodland path.[8]

His deep feeling and involvement with nature served as his constant analogy, sometimes simply descriptive:

Between the trees, the green sward slopes away,
  Barred with the sunshine, with the shadows crossed;
Where leaves, like flitting fingers, deftly play
  A melody, when by the breezee tossed.[9]

San Francisco, 1870

Sometimes as reflective of his search for an endless life:

Though the waves of death flow o'er thee,
  'Tis the rest that gathers power
For the endless life before thee:

Fear no dying;
Like the resurrection flower,
  Death defying.[10]

Salt Lake City, November 11, 1872

A significant part of the poetic expression of David Smith was in the field of music, a passion that was noticeable in early youth. He was just eighteen when he attended a prayer service in October 1863 at Manti, Iowa, with his brother Joseph; following a message from his older brother, he rose to sing "The Pebble Has Dropped in the Water" which went to the tune of *Faded Flowers*. This hymn holds a very traditional role in the Reorganization.

Let us shake off the coals from our garments
  And arise in the strength of our Lord
Let us break off the yoke of our bondage
  And be free in the joys of the world.
For the pebble has dropped in the water
  And the waves circle round with the shock --
Shall we anchor our barks in the center
  Or drift out and be wrecked on the rocks.[11]

1862

Known to many as the Sweet Singer of Israel, David often raised his powerful voice when other means of expression failed him; he wrote several hymns during his short productive life.

As for his talent as a painter and artist, we can say little, for the one or two works that remain at large are not sufficient to judge. His sketches are fairly common, for he left them with friends throughout the church and they have been saved. It was true, as his mother once remarked, "that he leaves sketches of flowers everywhere he goes."

The role of this young man as poet and artist awaits more formal analysis, as does the history of his life and his contribution. This brief comment is intended only to interest those more qualified to seek some insight into the life and thoughts of a man, torn by internal conformation, who felt he had a message but who could only write:

I would not sing, and yet I can not cease
I can not murmur, yet I have no peace[12]

PAUL EDWARDS

---

[1]David H. Smith and Elbert A. Smith, *Hesperis or Poems By Father and Son* (Herald Publishing House: Lamoni, Iowa, 1911), p. 226.
[2]*Saints' Herald*, II, 166.
[3]*The History of the Reorganized Church of Jesus Christ of Latter Day Saints*, III, 496. (Hereafter *RLDS History*)
[4]*Saints' Herald*, XVII, 180.
[5]*Brother Elbert* (Herald Publishing House: Independence, Missouri, 1959), pp. 11-14. (Revised from Elbert Smith, *On Memory's Beam* 1929.)
[6]*Book of Doctrine and Covenants* (Herald Publishing House: Independence, Missouri, 1962), section 117.3.
[7]*RLDS History*, IV, 460-469.
[8]David H. Smith, p. 126.
[9]*Ibid.*, p. 164.
[10]*Ibid.*, p. 171.
[11]*Ibid.*, p. 223.
[12]*Ibid.*, p. 226.

MORMON HYMNS

Of all the selections in *Hymns of the Church of Jesus Christ of Latter-day Saints,* only one third contain both text and music by Mormon authors and composers. One third consists of either text or music by members of the Church and one third is completely borrowed. This borrowing of texts and tunes from other Christian worshippers reflects a tradition of Mormons to reach out to all praiseworthy sources. The time is recurring, however, when Mormon composers and authors are feeling a resurgence of original expression. The Festivals have sought and performed many such works. Selected examples are published here and appear on the recording in this volume. They typify the quality, styles of writing, and religious sentiments of this second century of the restored Church. They are inspired by that revelation where the Lord says, "For my soul delighteth in the song of the heart; yea, the song of the righteous is a prayer unto me, and it shall be answered with a blessing upon their heads." D&C 25:12.

LORIN F. WHEELWRIGHT

FRANZ M. JOHANSEN, Artist

Prayer

Michael F. Moody

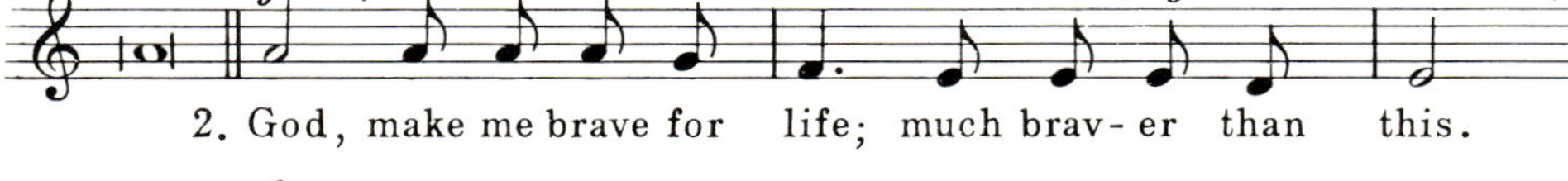

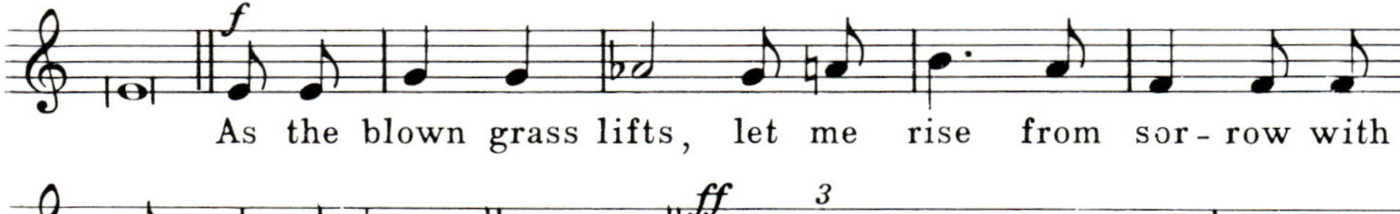

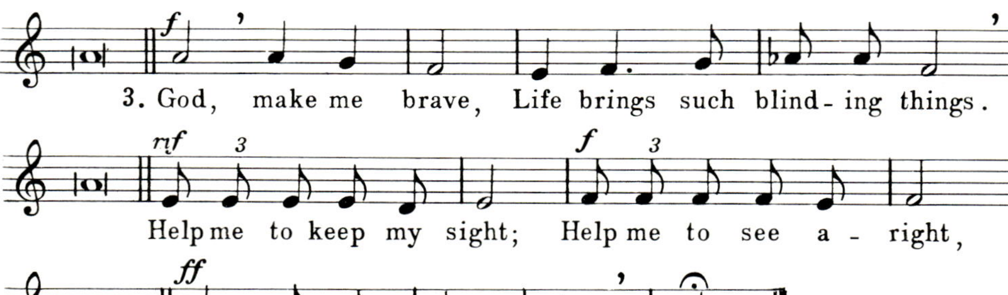

* Half of the congregation sings the words on these pitches.

Oh, Cruel Thorns

Words by
Onita Davis

Music by
Gaylen Hatton

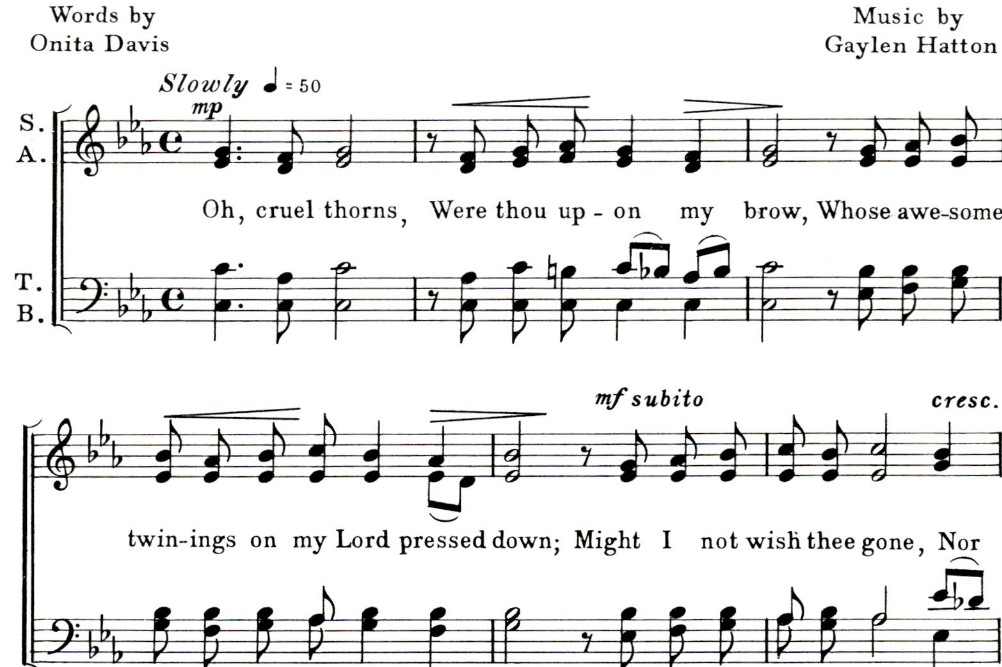

mp subito
f
hope to know   A sweet-er lot than death be-neath thy crown.
(♩.)

p
Thou pier-ced hands,   And bod-y wound-ed   sore;   The heart's blood

cresc.   f
spill-ing down as som-ber rain,   My heart and hands do re-as-

decresc.   mp   p
sure,   do re-as-sure,   do re-as-sure.   Those
sure,

cresc.   mf   mp
scar-let well-ing drops fall not in vain.   O pre-cious signs,

cresc. poco
So pure and un-de-filed,   Of ho-ly flesh and blood in

a poco   mf   cresc.
sac-ri-fice;   May I be-come in faith a lit-tle

f   mp
child,   Par-tak-ing guilt-less-ly be-fore His eyes.
(♩.)

p
And wear-y feet,   who paid thy fear-ful toll   Up-on the

cresc.   f
ston-y way to Cal-va-ry;   Set now thy prints up-on my

cresc. poco a poco al fine   walk in joy,   and I will
soul,   And I will   walk   in joy,   in
soul,
soul, And I   will

walk in joy,   And I will   allargando   ff
joy,   walk in joy to fol-low Thee!
joy, And I   will

MUSIC
IN CONCERT
AND THE THEATRE

The quality of a culture is determined by the taste that has been developed by that culture. Thus the attitude of a person toward the arts indicates his degree of artistic taste. Every Latter-day Saint should develop good taste in music. Through performing or listening to music of the concert stage, a person can gain an appreciation of the symphony orchestra, choral societies, chamber music, concert bands, operettas, musicals, chamber opera, grand opera, and the performing artists as well as the music of the theatre.

Where music is being performed, there is an aura of immediacy and excitement because of the visual, aural, mental, and emotional experiences that the listener beholds. If a live performance is not available, a true listening experience of high-fidelity stereo recordings or tape, and radio and/or television would be the next preferable source. Each Latter-day Saint has the resonsibility to expand his own musical understanding and cultural resources.

Acquiring sensitivity to the tonal materials of music is the challenge in developing good musical taste. Everyone has the capacity to enjoy music; consequently, every person should have the opportunity, as well as the obligation, to develop a high degree of excellence in his response to the best of musical sound. Music can give continual individual enrichment, relaxation, appreciation, and aesthetic experiences throughout life. The communication of emotion, meaning, and feeling through music expresses man's deepest self through the medium of live sounds. Through music each person can increase his ability to have aesthetic experiences on the highest plane. President David O. McKay said, "The opportunity for rising above the plane of animal existence is open to all who will choose it." The vast wealth of musical literature offers tremendous opportunities for continued cultural development.

May each Latter-day Saint seek out opportunities for musical participation, whether it be listening or performing, so that his life may be enriched by this great medium.

A. HAROLD GOODMAN

WALLACE M. BARRUS, *Photographer*

MUSIC
IN THE
MORMON HOME

Music glorifies the Mormon family. It is cradled where feelings are revered and members are sensitive to spiritual values. It is instrumental in lifting the human spirit above physical appetites and in arousing awe for the divine promise of life eternal. It touches the heart strings and ties them together in family harmony. Such is the role of music in the home of a Latter-day Saint family which truly seeks the spirit of Christ.

How does it happen? Wise parents provide children with exciting and fulfilling musical experiences. They buy instruments and furnish private instruction; they accompany children to their lessons and supervise home practice. They become an audience for home performance and a cheering section for public performance. They gather the family together in family prayer to teach the spiritual value of unity and mutual support of those who perform. They offer gentle criticism; they communicate gratitude.

A Mormon mother is usually the one to persist in such efforts, and with her love and prodding each child has the opportunity to discover his own musical capacity. She is often the one who accompanies children to concerts and introduces them to performers so that they can shake the hands that make the music.

When birthdays and holidays offer natural occasions for gifts, wise parents give music lessons, instruments, recordings, books, and concert tickets rather than meaningless toys. These gifts lead to new interests and personal development. They give each child a priceless opportunity to make music a part of his own life.

As the family meets in home evening, members perform. New songs are composed and taught; plans are made for use of music on family trips. Those who can perform well are encouraged to cheer the sick and the saddened by their musical gifts. Children begin to accompany home singing and to perform well enough to sing and play at church. Strong bonds of family love are woven with these golden sounds of song.

In this environment, aglow with spiritual values, the child of talent senses a special significance of music in his life. He moves beyond curiosity and romantic attachment into the rigors of serious study, practice, and self-discipline. Such an environment nurtures the future artists of our culture and brings great joy to the family, the Church, the community, and the nation.

In the Mormon home, the gifted are taught to develop talent as a God-given opportunity and obligation. They are taught to use such talent for building the kingdom of God on earth; they are instructed to shun the pollution that comes from degrading exploitation.

This happy approach to music, nurtured by loving parents, gives a priceless heritage to children. In the bosom of such a Mormon family are kindled warm emotions of love, kindness, humility, thanksgiving, and determination — all accompanied by strains of lingering melody that make doing and remembering a joy forever.

LORIN F. WHEELWRIGHT

O Love, That Glorifies Thy Son

Words and Music by
Lorin F. Wheelwright

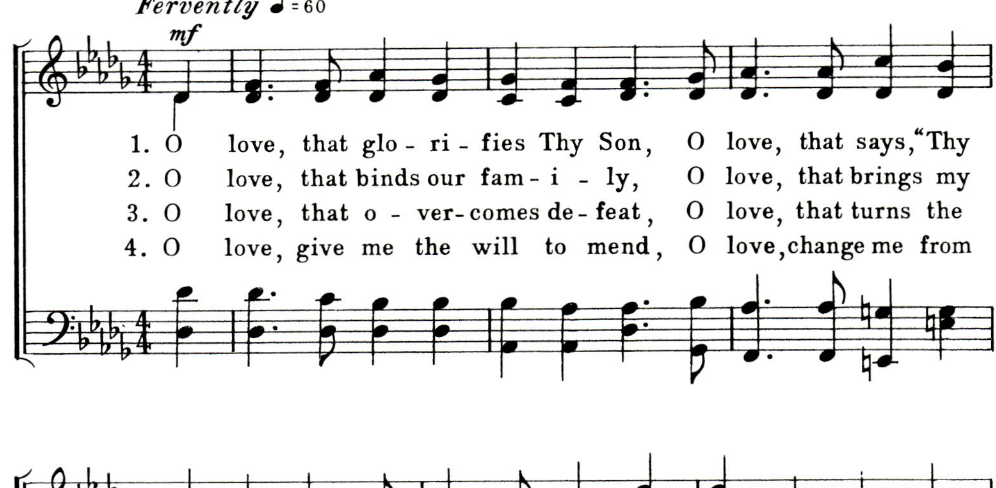

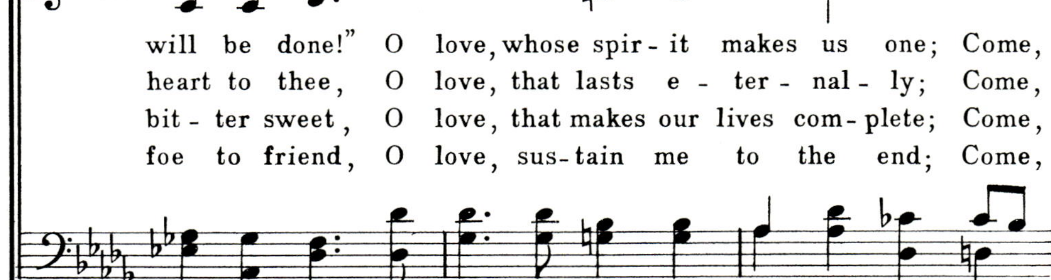

Copyright 1968 by Pioneer Music Press

O LOVE THAT GLORIFIES THY SON — This hymn, composed to be sung by families, was introduced by a group of eighty families, singing as one chorus, at the Salt Lake Tabernacle. Afterward, a young woman approached the composer and said, "A branch of my family is meeting. We have had harsh words. We need to heal wounded feelings. May we use your hymn?" Permission was gladly given, and a week later this young woman returned to express profound appreciation. She said, "After we sang this hymn and contemplated its meaning, the spirit of Christ entered our hearts and we solved our problems so easily we forgot that they were problems." Such can be the power of music in the home.

Oh, Love That Glorifies Thy Son appears on Mormon Arts Recording I, included with this volume.

MORMON BALLET FOREVER AND EVER

Forever and Ever is a thirty-minute dramatic ballet choreographed by the author to musical excerpts from *The Planets* by Gustav Holst. The story of the ballet states simply through classical ballet movement that a boy and girl meet; fall in love; are married for all time and eternity; and are separated because of war. The boy is killed in action; she mourns his death; then when she dies, they are reunited in the hereafter. The theme of the ballet originates from the Mormon value: love is eternal. Performance was given as a feature of the Second Annual Mormon Festival of Arts in 1970. Connie Burton and Howard Millet alternating with Paul Corrington performed the leads. The BYU Corps de Ballet assisted.

SANDRA B. ALLEN

BRENT HOLMES, Photographer

THE CREATIVE IMAGE OF PHOTOGRAPHY

We are all in the business of image making whether we tell a story with words, paint a picture with oils, or work with a lens and film. The images we create become our communications; they tell what we see and how we feel. Photography is a dramatic link in this image making. Everything on our television screens first goes through a lens. Someone selects and edits. Every picture in our publications is photographed at some point.

No longer is fine art creative and photography imitative. The dichotomy is false. Art in any form can be either imitative or creative. At Brigham Young University we seek to be creative. The photographer composes, selects, edits, and prints. He works with all manner of subjects and with editorial viewpoint. He wants you, the viewer, to complete his pictures by imagining what extends beyond the scene, what causes the action, what ensues from all you see. But more, he wants you to enjoy the experience. He wants you to relish the composition, the flow, the textures, and the full expression of tonal values.

All of his photography means nothing unless you, the viewer, leap into the picture, interact with all that is there, and come away different for having been there. When this happens you know you have fallen under the spell of a photographer whose images involve you in a joint creative enterprise.

LORIN F. WHEELWRIGHT

LOGAN TEMPLE — The temples of the Mormon Church have a celestial mystery about them. Even when one has been through the temple many times, he wonders if he understands the significance of even a tenth of the happenings within those spired buildings. I have stood outside several of our temples and felt strangely moved — not just inspired — by a kind of curious wonder. These temples represent, in their physical structure alone, all eternity and the fulness and glory of God — if we could but decipher the message, the code, and the feeling in the heart. This picture repeats the preceding statement to me: the foggy grey, the partial view of the structure, the bright circle of sunlight — all seem visually to hint at the mystery of heaven.

DON O. THORPE, Photographer

(This picture was a Purchase Award Winner in the 1971 Mormon Festival of Arts.)

Mormon Perceptions

A boy receiving ordination to the priesthood, a Scout winning his star rank, a dinner for a newly released bishopric, a ground breaking for a new ward chapel — these familiar events, so frequent in The Church of Jesus Christ of Latter-day Saints, are the special challenge of the Mormon photographer. How does he see them with a fresh eye, record them with a unique view? The talented photographer solves that problem by discovering the aesthetic dimension of these common events; in so doing, he lifts his work to an artistic level.

Church publications print trite photographs only when they have no others. Their editors encourage the free-lance or amateur photographer to submit photographs to them picturing any Church subject. They will pay for, print, and credit those that are pertinent and artistic.

Such photographers might follow the professional's practice of "serendipity" — the exploitation of unexpected opportunity. Professionals habitually carry a camera and habitually shoot more, not fewer, frames. One photographer chanced to visit a famous LDS family while carrying only his Polaroid camera. He was handicapped without his professional equipment, of course, but nevertheless he took a full series of photos. One week later the father died. Those pictures were published, displayed at the funeral, and earned the lasting gratitude of the family.

PRESIDENT DAVID O. MCKAY — **Beloved leader of the Mormon Church, President McKay, with his two counselors — Nathan E. Tanner and Hugh B. Brown — assisting him, makes a noble subject for a photographer. The significance of photography is found in the enjoyment of trying to obtain "the perfect picture." (If such is ever to be found.) Still, it provides the challenge and the demand of what Ansel Adams calls "a magnificent craft and science" — a continuing challenge to capture on film that perfect picture.**

BRUCE L. CHRISTENSEN, *Photographer*

An artistic, visual record of the Church has never been made. Where is the aesthetic visualization of Church documents, of the Mormon family, of the sacrament service, of the courts of honor, of a girl's Beehive years, of the Junior Sunday School? Where is an artful portfolio on any LDS gospel topic such as eternal

75

RALPH WATKINS STORY — "In our speed to laugh at others let us look at ourselves." — Todd Tobler, photographer of the Ralph Watkins story gives insight to the viewpoint behind the lens. This series of four pictures tells a story that commands not only photographic skill but spiritual origins. They help us understand that every man must in someway meet his Gethsemane. For some it is spiritual; for others it is mental; for still others it is physical. How one meets his particular Gethsemane is the crux of his life. We admire those who live successfully with their handicaps.

Ralph Watkins is a lad who is happier than most people who have no physical handicaps. He carries out his duties as a paper boy, passes the sacrament, and enjoys other activities of boys his age despite the fact that he was stricken at an early age with cerebral palsy. Ralph still has lonely moments. "They still tease me, but they don't understand," he says. After the example Ralph sets of overcoming his handicap, there are those who just begin to show theirs.

TODD TOBLER, Photographer

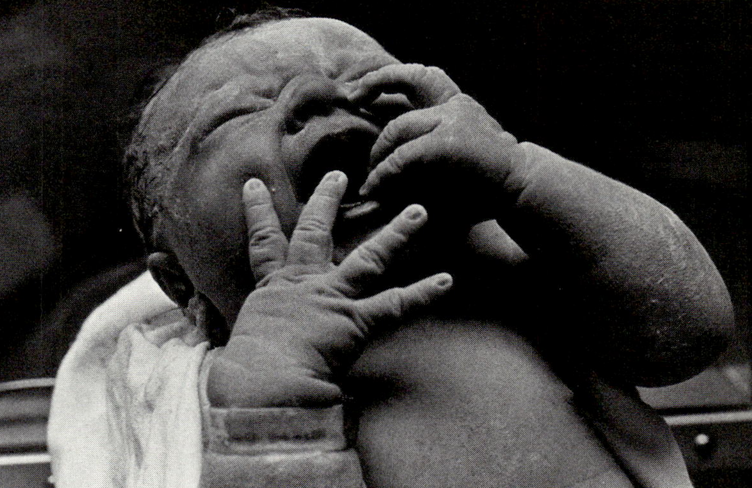

CRYING CHILD, by John Telford, page 80
MOTHER'S LOVE, by John Telford, left
HENRY AND ME, by D. Errol Miller, upper right
JENNIFER, 20 MINUTES OLD, by Bruce L. Christensen

Photography is dramatic image making. The master behind the camera wants you, the viewer, to complete his pictures by responding to the emotions he feels as he creates them. He wants you to interact with all the elements involved and come away different. He wants you to share a joint, creative venture. As you view the face of a crying child or see that child comforted in the arms of her mother, something happens. Perhaps a feeling for the importance of a mother's love gains new meaning. Seeing a newborn infant may stir new hope for a better world; seeing old people affirm the Mormon way of life may emphasize the value of deeds well done and work accomplished. Would a chicken stand on just anybody's shoulder?

ALLEN CORNWALL

Mormon chapel for the Second Stake, Utah State University, Logan, Utah, exemplifies recent architectural innovations in chapel design.

GOOD ENVIRONMENT BALANCES SELF WITH OTHERS

Latter-day Saints place a high premium upon personal progress and the common good. Where these two motives clash, as they may seem to do in certain practices regarding the management of our environment, President David O. McKay placed the highest priority upon the spiritual principle of unselfishness. He said in general conference, "Specifically stated, this law is, 'We live our lives most completely when we strive to make the world better and happier.' The law of pure nature, survival of the fittest, is self-preservation at the sacrifice of all else; but in contrast to this law of spiritual life is, *deny the self for the good of others.*" (Emphasis added.)[1]

In the rich tradition of the Saints, the Mormon people have tamed a wilderness to make a desert blossom as the rose. They have built homes and encouraged pride of ownership through frugality, maintenance, and improvement. Brigham Young instructed the pioneers one hundred years ago to fix the garden fence, fix the yard and make it look neater . . . fix the house and make it more convenient.[2] President John Taylor inspired Latter-day Saints to believe that "we shall rear splendid edifices, magnificent temples and beautiful cities that shall become the pride, praise and glory of the whole earth."[3]

Today these admonitions and promises have only partially come to pass. The ugly slovenliness, pollution, and desecration of man's habitat are shocking us into the realization that prophetic fulfillment depends on our own efforts. Not only is our collective conscience stricken by failure to act on high principles, but our physical and spiritual health is being jeopardized by our environmental neglect.

The Mormon Festival of Arts focused attention on these problems. In symposium discussion these points were made:

1. *Clean* is a word that suggests power of environment over mind.

2. Architectural eclecticism has not always stamped our efforts with noble purpose.

3. Unless we see the larger view of the earth as a whole, we just continue to paint over and fix up.

4. Correct home designs tend to stress appearance rather than function and to follow fads rather than deeply felt necessities.

5. Our individual tastes have exceeded our purse. We now must establish a priority of values in terms of spiritual needs.

6. High in the priority of spiritual values is *honesty* of design, not merely "authentic" imitations devoid of modern conveniences nor "rabbit warrens" to put roofs over heads. We need designs of homes and public structures to provide for privacy and projection of high aspiration.

7. Some Latter-day Saints tend to stress interior housekeeping and neglect exterior housekeeping.

8. Population mobility is currently dictating designs of homes to meet a resale market. To achieve architectural independence, homeowners need financial independence or highly creative solutions for personal design problems. Design solutions may lie in current trends toward modular construction suitable for inexpensive rearrangement to meet the needs of subsequent owners.

9. The architectural policies of the Church in chapel building stress functional use of space for worship, teaching, and recreation, devoid of frills or vain ornamentation.

10. As public policy we need to assess historical structures that embody high spiritual purpose and preserve the best as models to inspire future architectural integrity.

11. Latter-day Saints, by tradition and principle, should set an example to the world that environmental virtue begins at home. Rather than rely upon political pressures, we should seek to clean up our own yards, rebuild our own fences, preserve the best of our own private and public buildings. Thus, by example, we can demonstrate that each person is responsible for making this a better world in which to live.

WHY?

PROGRESS. . .
It destroys the meanderings of a river,
    Making it straight and narrow.
    Why? . . . to control floods!
It blasts away the coral shelf of a hundred billion
    cells,
    Glistening in the sea for fifty million years.
    Why? . . . so ships can berth!
It slashes a gash in the desert sands,
    Whose wrinkles smile and frown with the
    seasons.
    Why? . . . to speed deliveries!
It plows a waterway through the land,
    Like a tracheotomy of a continent.
    Why? . . . so commerce can breathe.
It pierces the mountain with a tunneled tube,
    Where blank walls hide the alpine vistas.
    Why? . . . so traffic can flow.
It demolishes ten thousand homes.
    Where children play and hearths are warm.
    Why? . . . so water can be stored.
It fells a giant tree a century old,
    Leaving an aching wound in the sky and the
    heart.
    Why? . . .so a new house can be built.

PROGRESS is the excuse;
    . . . but the reason?
    Time means death.
    Time means life.
    Time runs out.
    Time is power.
    Power is glory.
    AMEN!

LORIN F. WHEELWRIGHT, *Author Photographer*

Early Mormon rock houses are being restored in Pleasant Grove, Utah. Under reconstruction is a home built by Alfred Harper in 1876. By removing side shingles and stucco, the original square-cut stone, hewn from American Fork Canyon, is revealed. The completely restored home with added balcony is the Driggs home, formerly occupied by the King Driggs family who are known as the King Family on television.

The old log cabin is typical of early pioneer structures in need of restoration and preservation.

Good houses are comfortable and very convenient, and please our feelings. . . . If you wish to build a house, build as good a one as you can imagine.

Brigham Young, May 1855

Let every individual in this city feel the same interest for the public good as he does for his own, and you will see at once this community still more prosperous and still more rapidly increasing in wealth, influence, and power. But where one seeks to benefit himself or herself alone, and doesn't cherish a feeling for the prosperity and benefit of the whole, that people will be disorderly, unhappy, and poverty striken, and distress, animosity, and strife will reign.

Orson Pratt

We believe that we shall rear splendid edifices, magnificent temples and beautiful cities that shall become the pride, praise, and glory of the whole earth . . . and we shall have eventually, when, the Lord's purposes are carried out, the most pleasant and beautiful gardens. Zion will become the praise of the whole earth.

John Taylor, *Journal of Discourses*, April 1863

Specifically stated, this law is, "We live our lives most completely when we strive to make the world better and happier." The law of pure nature, survival of the fittest, is self-preservation at the sacrifice of all else; but in contrast to this the law of spiritual life is deny the self for the good of others.

There never was a time in the history of the world when the application of this principle was more needed. Therefore, let sincere men and women the world over unite in earnest effort to supplant feelings of selfishness, hatred, animosity, greed, by the law of service to others, and thereby promote the peace and happiness of mankind.

David O. McKay, April 1936

There is a word that has within it some wonderful possibilities for personal peace, for safety, for self-respect, and the word is called "clean." Clean hands, clean hearts, clean homes, clean water, clean air, clean clothes — clean minds, clean morals — what a wonderful word! The mind so often follows the environment — and the cycle reverses itself, as environment follows the mind.

Richard L. Evans, "The Spoken Word," November 1969

(Quotations Courtesy of Milo Baughman,
BYU Environmental Design Department)

COALVILLE TABERNACLE, D. Errol Miller, *Photographer*

FIRST ANNUAL MORMON FESTIVAL OF ARTS

April 28 through May 3, 1969

Art Exhibit
Invitational exhibition of painting and sculpture by Mormon artists from across the nation. Directed by Dale T. Fletcher. B.F. Larson Art Gallery.

Symposium on Mormon Art
Directed by Dale T. Fletcher

American Premiere: *Pilgrim's Progress*
A morality opera by Ralph Vaughan Williams, founded on Bunyan's allegory of the same title.

SECOND ANNUAL MORMON FESTIVAL OF ARTS

March 18 through April 30, 1970

Mormon Tabernacle Choir Concert
March 18
A memorable evening of LDS favorites, including a musical tribute to David O. McKay, entitled "The Gentle Way," by Robert Cundick. Choir was conducted by Richard P. Condie. Smith Fieldhouse, 8:15 p.m. Thirty-five hundred attended.

Spring Ballet Concert
March 18 through March 21
The Brigham Young University Corps de Ballet in a colorful evening of dance, featuring an original Mormon ballet, *Forever and Ever.* This was conceived and choreographed by Sandra Allen and based on the Mormon philosophy that love and temple marriage are eternal. Soloists: Paul Corrington, Howard Millett, Connie Burton, and Caroline Prohoski, assisted by the BYU Corps de Ballet of thirty.

Retrospective Art Exhibit
March 18 through April 30
Outstanding Mormon art of the past. B.F. Larsen Gallery, Harris Fine Arts Center, 8:00 a.m. to 10:00 p.m. daily.

Contemporary Art Exhibit
March 18 through April 30
The best of today's Mormon art. Forty pieces from approximately 120 submitted on display. B.F. Larsen Gallery, Harris Fine Arts Center, 8:00 a.m. to 10:00 p.m. daily.

Music in the Home Workshop
March 19
Directed by D. Evan Davis with Dr. Rendal Gibbons as chairman. Participants included Percy Kalt and family; Dr. Robert Downs and family; and Dr. Darrel Stubbs and family. Madsen Recital Hall, Harris Fine Arts Center, 10:00 a.m. to noon.

Chamber Music Concert
March 19
Small ensembles and a quintet, featuring new works by Mormon composers. One hundred fifty attended. Madsen Recital Hall, Harris Fine Arts Center, 2:00 p.m.

Viola Recital: David Dalton
March 19
Paul Pollei, pianist assisting. Performing works by Fuerstner, Barbirolli, Britten, and Mardis. Two hundred twenty-five attended. Madsen Recital Hall, Harris Fine Arts Center, 4:00 p.m.

Choral Concert: Oratorio Choir and Symphony Orchestra
March 19
With Dr. John R. Halliday conducting, the performance included "Faure Requiem" and "Ode to Libertad" by La Mar Barrus. Soloists were Colleen Eads, *soprano,* and Arden Hopkins, *baritone.* De Jong Concert Hall, Harris Fine Arts Center, 8:15 p.m. Fourteen hundred attended.

Symposium: Music in the LDS Worship Service
March 20
Panel and workshop. Dr. Clifford Barnes, BYU, moderator; Parley Belnap, BYU organist; Dr. Robert Cundick, Tabernacle organist; Dr. Alma Ditner, Utah State University; Dr. William Foxley, BYU faculty; J.J. Keeler, BYU organist; Dr. Alexander Schreiner, senior Tabernacle organist; Dr. Lorin F. Wheelwright, dean of the College of Fine Arts, BYU. Madsen Recital Hall, Harris Fine Arts Center, 10:00 a.m. One hundred attended.

Chamber Music Recital
March 20
String quartet and woodwind quintet, Madsen Recital Hall, Harris Fine Arts Center, 2:00 p.m. One hundred twenty-five attended.

Piano Recital: Michael Cannon
March 20
Madsen Recital Hall, Harris Fine Arts Center, 4:00 p.m. Two hundred fifty attended.

A Cappella Choir Concert
March 20
Featured the works of ten Utah composers. Ralph Woodward, conducting. De Jong Concert Hall, Harris Fine Arts Center, 8:15 p.m. Twelve hundred attended.

The LDS Musician as a Professional
March 21
Panel discussion with LDS musicians. Dr. Reid Nibley, moderator. Madsen Recital Hall, Harris Fine Arts Center, 10:00 a.m. Seventy-five attended.

Vocal Recital: Ray Arbizu, Operatic Tenor
March 21
Madsen Recital Hall, Harris Fine Arts Center, 2:00 p.m. One hundred twenty-five attended.

BYU Philharmonic Orchestra Concert
March 21
Conducted by Prof. Lawrence Sardoni. Performance of Beethoven's Seventh Symphony and music by LDS composers. De Jong Concert Hall, Harris Fine Arts Center, 8:15 p.m. Eight hundred attended.

Faculty Chamber Recital
March 23
De Jong Concert Hall, Harris Fine Arts Center, 8:15 p.m. One hundred attended.

Young Writers of the Church
March 23
Selected works of young LDS authors. 184 Jesse Knight Building, 7:00 to 9:00 p.m.

Writing and Publishing in the Church Symposium
March 24
Principal editors of Church publications. 184 Jesse Knight Building, 4:00 p.m.

W-2 Form: Dramatic Presentation
March 25-28, 30-31; April 1-2
Experimental play written and directed by Dr. Lael Woodbury, assistant dean, College of Fine Arts and Communications, BYU. Margetts Arena Theatre, Harris Fine Arts Center, 8:15 p.m. Attended by 1,173.

Leonard Penario: Piano Concert
March 25
Lyceum presentation, de Jong Concert Hall, Harris Fine Arts Center, 8:15 p.m. Attended by 1,451.

The Literature of the Church
March 25
Highlights and excerpts from some of the best Church literature. 184 Jesse Knight Building, 7:30 p.m.

I Remember Mama: Dramatic Presentation
March 26-28, 30-31; April 1,2
Nostalgic family comedy by John Van Druten; directed by Dr. Preston Gledhill. Pardoe Drama Theatre, Harris Fine Arts Center, 1:30 p.m. Forty-six hundred attended.

Faculty Chamber Recital
March 30
De Jong Concert Hall, Harris Fine Arts Center, 8:15 p.m.

Symposium on Mormon Art
April 1
Directed by Dale T. Fletcher, BYU Art Department. Mormon artists should interpret their heritage. Panel members included Dale T. Fletcher, A. Valoy Eaton, Ross Johnson, and John Morgan. Also presented a film, *Stone Man,* produced by Rell Francis. Nelke Experimental Theatre, Harris Fine Arts Center, 2:00 p.m.

Chamber Choir Concert
April 1
Madsen Recital Hall, Harris Fine Arts Center, 8:15 p.m.

Dramatic Mormon Vignettes
April 1, 2
Winning entries of sketches based on real life characters and events in Mormon history. Nelke Experimental Theatre, Harris Fine Arts Center, 7:00 p.m.

Bishops' and Stake Presidents' Day
April 2
Welcome to LDS leaders to the BYU campus. Special production by the College of Fine Arts, *A House of the Lord,* portraying the rise and fall of Kirtland Temple. Smith Fieldhouse, 10:00 a.m.

Utah Symphony Concert
April 10
De Jong Concert Hall, Harris Fine Arts Center, 8:15 p.m.

Seminar in Organ Pedagogy
April 11
Workshop/seminar for Church organists. Madsen Recital Hall, Harris Fine Arts Center, 10:00 a.m.

Organ Recital
April 11
Provo Tabernacle, downtown Provo, 2:00 p.m.

Pilgrim's Progress
April 20, 22, 23, 24, 25
Opera, de Jong Concert Hall, Harris Fine Arts Center, 8:15 p.m.

A Cappella Choir
April 30
With Ralph Woodward, de Jong Concert Hall, Harris Fine Arts Center, 8:15 p.m.

THIRD ANNUAL MORMON FESTIVAL OF ARTS

March 17 Through April 2, 1971

Invitational Art Exhibits
Wednesday, March 17 - Friday, April 2
Invitational exhibits of LDS artists from across the nation. Directed by Dale Fletcher. $500 purchase prize. C.C.A. Christensen Mormon Panorama, B.F. Larsen Art Gallery. Floyd Breinholt exhibition, Secured Gallery. Attendance: 25,000.

Invitational Mormon Photography
Wednesday, March 17 - Friday, April 2
Prints in color and black and white that express Mormon values. Directed by Wallace M. Barrus. A $100 purchase prize. B.F. Larsen Art Gallery. Attendance: 25,000.

Motion Picture: Man's Search for Happiness
Wednesday, March 17
A special Japanese version, directed by W.O. Whitaker. 3:00 p.m., Nelke Experimental Theatre. Attendance: 70.

Musical: *The Order Is Love*
Wednesday, March 17 - Saturday, March 20
An original Mormon musical that combines the idealism of the united order with the nostalgia of young love. Directed by Max C. Golightly; book by Carol Lynn Pearson; music by Alexis de Azevedo. 8:00 p.m., de Jong Concert Hall. Attendance: 6,883.

Mormon Vignettes
Thursday, March 18; Friday, March 19; Thursday, March 25; Friday, March 26
Dramatic sketches of Mormon personalities. Supervised by Charles W. Whitman; directed by Gerald Argetsinger. 5:00 p.m., Nelke Experimental Theatre. Attendance: 600.

Play: *The Apostate*
Thursday, March 18 - Friday, April 2
An original drama, by Orson Scott Card, relating the conflict of Alma, the younger, with his family. Directed by Charles W. Whitman. 8:00 p.m., Margetts Arena Theatre. Attendance: 2,000.

BYU Touring Repertory Theatre: *Hamlet*
Friday, March 19 - Saturday, March 20
Special performance by the permanent cast of sixteen actors. Directed by Dr. Harold I. Hansen. 6:00 p.m., Pardoe Drama Theatre. Attendance: 2,458.

BYU Touring Repertory Theatre: *The Tragedy of Korihor*
Friday, March 19 - Saturday, March 20
Written by Mrs. Louise Hanson. The story of the tragedy of Korihor is taken from the Book of Mormon, Alma 30:6-60. Directors: Jean Jenkins and Dr. Harold I. Hansen. 8:00 p.m., Pardoe Drama Theatre. Attendance: 2,458.

Symposium on Mormon Arts and History
Saturday, March 20
Mormon History Association conducted a discussion on the works of David A. Smith and significant Mormon music. Supervised by James B. Allen. Participants: Paul Edwards, Graceland College in Lamoni, Iowa; William E. Berret, BYU. Attendance: 80.

Symposium on Mormon Photography
Monday, March 22
Chairman: Wallace M. Barrus. 1:00 p.m. 321 Ernest L. Wilkinson Center.

Symposium on Mormon Art
Monday, March 22
Chairman: Dale T. Fletcher. 3:00 p.m., E-400 Harris Fine Arts Center. Attendance: 110.

Faculty Solo and Chamber Music Concert
Monday, March 22
A model program for LDS ward and stake music evenings. Supervised by E.H. Powley. 8:15 p.m., Madsen Recital Hall. Attendance: 300.

Literature Symposium: "Bishops, Blood, and Bandits: The Mormon Image for the Non-Mormon Writer"
Tuesday, March 23
The Mormon image in popular and sophisticated literature of Europe and of nineteenth- and twentieth-century America. 3:00 p.m., 321 Ernest L. Wilkinson Center. Attendance: 95.

Creative Dramatics: "The Development of Self-Expression"
Wednesday, March 24
Demonstration by children; short lecture by Dr. Calvin Taylor (University of Utah); and a panel discussion treating the subject "Keeping Creative Dramatics Creative." Supervisor: Robert E. Struthers. Directed by Mrs. Audra Moss, Orem, Utah. 3:00 p.m., Nelke Experimental Theatre. Attendance: 90.

Three-Screen Slide Show with Sound
Wednesday, March 24
Autumn in Aspen Grove, southern Utah's majestic scenery, Lake Powell, and Temple Square as photographed by Mr. Sharrol T. Felt of BYU Motion Picture Studio. Supervised by Wallace Barrus. 3:00 p.m., Nelke Experimental Theatre. Attendance: 60.

Oratorio: Mendelssohn's *Elijah*
Thursday, March 25

One of the musical masterpieces of the world performed by the BYU Oratorio Choir and Philharmonic Orchestra. Dr. John R. Halliday, conducting. 8:15 p.m., de Jong Concert Hall. Attendance: 1,420.

Design and Ecology
Friday, March 26
Environmental symposium including a panel discussion, a sound-slide presentation, live music, and readers. Milo Baughman, chairman. 2:00 p.m., Nelke Experimental Theatre.

Mormon Values and Environment
Friday, March 26
On stage exhibit plus two short sound films: *This is Provo* and *Environmental Design and Mormon Values*. Milo Baughman, chairman. 8:00 p.m., Madsen Recital Hall.

Wind Symphony
Friday, March 26
Music by LDS composers of Nauvoo and early Salt Lake City as played by the unusual Wind Symphony. Directed by Dr. Ralph G. Laycock. 8:15 p.m., de Jong Concert Hall. Attendance: 882.

Organ Recital: Dr. Robert Cundick
Saturday, March 27
Part one, concert selections; part two, new organ music suitable for LDS worship services. Supervisor of event: E.H. Powley. 8:15 p.m., Madsen Recital Hall. Attendance: 375.

Easter Fireside Program
Sunday, March 28
Supervised by Dr. A. Harold Goodman. 7:00 p.m., Smith Fieldhouse.

Photography in LDS Church
Monday, March 29
Panel discussion by outstanding Mormon photographers on the creative image and the quality of photography in the Church. Supervised by Wallace M. Barrus. 3:00 p.m., 321 Ernest L. Wilkinson Center.

I Want to Write
Monday, March 29
An evening with Mormon student writers who will read original poems and fiction on LDS themes. Supervised by Richard Cracroft. 8:00 p.m., Madsen Recital Hall. Attendance: 175.

Piano Recital: Dr. Reid Nibley
Monday, March 29
An evening of music which might serve as a guide for an LDS home evening program. Supervised by E.H. Powley. 8:15 p.m., de Jong Concert Hall. Attendance: 543.

Religious Expression through the Art of Dance
Monday, March 29
Original works as choreographed by BYU dance faculty. Supervised by Sara Lee Gibb. 8:15 p.m., 185 Richards Building. Attendance: 550.

The Arts as a Proselyting Tool
Tuesday, March 30
Panel discussion on the role played by the Mormon Tabernacle Choir, Hill Cumorah Pageant, Church information centers, etc., in affecting attitudes toward the Church. Supervised by H.R. Oaks. 3:10 p.m., Nelke Experimental Theatre.

Music in the Mormon Home
Wednesday, March 31
Demonstration and discussion of the problem of performing, teaching, and enjoying music in the LDS home. Supervised by Dr. D. Evan Davis. Participants: Dr. J.E. Welch, University of Utah, Music Faculty; Dr. Reid Nibley, BYU Music Faculty; Dr. Clark Webb, BYU, Music Faculty. Attendance: 200.

On The Threshold
Wednesday, March 31
Some prominent Mormon poets read their works. Supervised by Richard Cracroft. 8:00 p.m., Nelke Experimental Theatre. Attendance: 300.

Philharmonic Orchestra Concert
Wednesday, March 31
Yoshie Akimota, pianist. Dr. Ralph G. Laycock, conductor. New music, by LDS composers, written for symphony orchestra. 8:15 p.m., de Jong Concert Hall. Attendance: 1,381.

Musical Compositions Suitable for the LDS worship service
Thursday, April 1
Panel discussion and demonstration of suitable techniques in composing Church hymns and other musical works suitable for the LDS worship service. Supervised by Dr. A. Harold Goodman. 3:10 p.m., Madsen Recital Hall. Attendance: 100.

BYU A Cappella Choir Choral Concert
Thursday, April 1
Concert of secular and sacred music by LDS composers. Directed by Fred Webb. 8:15 p.m., de Jong Concert Hall. Attendance: 812.

Bishops' and Stake Presidents' Assembly
Friday, April 2
Mormon Panorama with projected art, dialogue, and music. Supervised by Dr. A. Harold Goodman. Directed by Dr. Merrill Bradshaw. Attendance: 6,304.

BIOGRAPHICAL SKETCHES

ALLEN, SANDRA B.; p. 73

333 West 100 North, Provo, Utah 84601
B.: Salt Lake City, Utah; September 8, 1942. BFA, University of Utah, 1964; MFA, University of Utah, 1966; performed as a soloist with University of Utah Theatre in roles ranging from children's parts to demisoloist in *Waltz of the Flowers* and *Merliton*, soloist in *Arabian* and *Mechanical Doll*.

ANDRUS, J. ROMAN; p. 4

1765 North 651 East, Provo, Utah 84601
B.: St. George, Utah; July 11, 1907. B.S., BYU; M.S., BYU; Ed.D., University of Colorado; studied under Ralph Holmes, Edward Vysekal, Frederick Taubes; teacher, BYU. Otis Faculty Award of Merit; Distinguished Service Award from the Utah Academy of Sciences; Excellence in Art award from the Arts Council of Central Utah. Exhibits: California, Utah, Massachusetts, New York, Kansas, and numerous one-man shows.

BAILEY, ALICE MORREY; p. 51

1456 Edison Street, Salt Lake City, Utah 84111
B.: Joseph, Utah; August 21, 1903. Studied at BYU, University of Utah. Poet of the year, Utah State Poetry Society. Published works: "Eden from an Appleseed"; numerous plays; short stories and poems in *Relief Society Magazine*.

BARRUS, WALLACE McBRIDE; pp. 29, 41, 52, 54-61, 70, 71

1311 North 380 West, Provo, Utah 84601
B.: Salt Lake City, Utah; June 5, 1930. B.S., BYU; completing MFA degree in art, with a discipline in photography, Utah State University; commercial photographer; Director of Photography, Department of Motion Picture Production, BYU; instructor of photography, BYU.

BIRD, RICHARD EUGENE; pp. 39, 53, 61

Rexburg, Idaho
B.: Glendale, Arizona; September 19, 1937. A.A., Ricks College; B.S., Utah State University; MFA, BYU, 1971; illustrator for Thiokol Chemical Corp.; art director for Trailwide Corp., Oxnard, California; director of advertising and design for Chart-A-Matic Corp., Orem, Utah; free-lance artist; teaching assistantship, BYU, 1969-71; art director, Ricks College.

BRADSHAW, MERRILL; p. 69

248 East 3140 North, Provo, Utah 84601
B.: Lyman, Wyoming; June 18, 1929. A.B., BYU, 1954; M.A., BYU, 1955; M.Mus., University of Illinois, 1956; D.Mus.A., University of Illinois, 1962; coordinator of applied music at BYU, 1962-67; 37 works performed.

BREINHOLT, FLOYD E.; pp. 35, 51

1135 North Cherry Lane, Provo, Utah 84601
B.: Ephraim, Utah; December 25, 1915. Graduate of Snow College, 1935; B.S., BYU, 1937; M.E., BYU, 1953; teacher, Manti Jr. High School, Manti, Utah, and Farrer Jr. High School, Provo, Utah; principal, Joaquin Elementary School, Provo, Utah; principal, Central Jr. High School, Provo, Utah, 1956-61; associate professor of art, BYU, since 1961.

BULLOUGH, ROBERT V.; pp. 2, 65

3468 Santa Rosa Drive, Salt Lake City, Utah 84109
B.: Seattle, Washington; January 12, 1926. Teacher, Granite School District; free-lance illustrator; painter and sculptor; teacher, University of Utah.

BURNSIDE, WESLEY M.; p. 50

605 Sagewood Road, Provo, Utah 84601
B.: Mount Pleasant, Utah; November 16, 1918. B.S., BYU, 1941; M.S., BYU, 1949; Ph.D., Ohio State University, 1970; associate professor, Art Department, BYU. Exhibits: Idaho; traveling show in Pacific Northwest; several one-man shows.

CHEESMAN, PAUL R.; p. 32

344 South 350 East, Orem, Utah
B.: Brigham City, Utah; May 31, 1921. B.A., San Diego State College; M.A., BYU; Ph.D., BYU; graduate school, UCLA, University of Miami; President, Professional Photographers of America, San Diego; teacher, BYU.

CHRISTENSEN, BRUCE L.; pp. 75, 76, 77, 81

364 Stadium Circle, Provo, Utah 84601
B.: Ogden, Utah; April 26, 1943. B.A., University of Utah; MSJ, Northwestern University; statehouse reporter, KSL News; news director, KNUR; sports writer-producer, WGN Television, Director, Broadcast Services, BYU.

CHRISTENSEN, JAMES C.; p. 15

521A East Mill Street, Santa Maria, California 93454
B.: Culver City, California. M.A., BYU, 1968; instructor of art, Fester Jr. High School, Santa Maria, California.

CORNABEY, FLOYD V.; p. 28

18151 Gleada Street, Huntington Beach, California 92646
B.: Spanish Fork, Utah; July 4, 1910. B.S., BYU; M.A., Columbia University; Chairman, Art Department, Utah State University; chairman of art departments of three Huntington Beach high schools; teacher, Orange Coast College.

CORNWALL, ALLEN S.; pp. 44, 50, 81

2174 Yuma Street, Salt Lake City, Utah 84109
B.: Salt Lake City, Utah; January 6, 1927. B.A., University of Utah; graduate work, UCLA, BYU; teacher, BYU; assistant to dean, College of Fine Arts, BYU; copywriter, KUTV; television director, KUTV; copywriter, Ross Jurney & Assoc.; editor, *Music Life Magazine*; owner, Corlan Advertising Agency.

DARAIS, ALEX B., pp. 3, 42-43

1835 North 500 East, Provo, Utah 84601
B.: Santa Monica, California; April 4, 1918. B.A., BYU, 1948; MFA, Pomona Associated College, 1952; assistant professor, Art Department, BYU. Exhibits: one-man shows in California and Utah.

DE AZAVEDO, ALEXIS K.; p. 53

17230 Gresham St., Northridge, California 91324
B.: Los Angeles, California; January 14, 1943. Capitol Records 1965-68: producer-arranger for: Laurindo Almeida, Mrs. Miller, Human Beinz, Lettermen, George Shearing, Jody Miller, Four Preps, Esquivel, Hollyridge Strings, King Sisters, King Family, Ray Anthony, Kay Starr, and others; Live television: Hollywood Palace, Kraft Music Hall, Jonathon Winters, King Family Show, 1969, Robert Young CBS Special.

DIXON, JANICE THORNE; p. 61

4806 Quail Point Road, Salt Lake City, Utah 84110
B.: Provo, Utah; May 9, 1932. B.A., M.A., University of Utah. Published works: "Mormon Vignettes," *Relief Society Magazine*; "Halloween Play," *Grade School Teacher Magazine*.

EATON, A. VALOY; p. 8.

4178 Annapolis Drive, Salt Lake City, Utah 84120
B.: Vernal, Utah; March 29, 1938. B.A., BYU, 1960; M.A., BYU, 1971; teacher, Granite School District; awards in various local, regional, and national exhibits. Exhibits: one-man shows, Utah, Illinois; Pennsylvania.

EDWARDS, PAUL M.; p. 65

Lamoni, Iowa
B.: Independence, Missouri; February 26, 1933. M.A., University of South Dakota; Ph.D., University of St. Andrews, Scotland, 1971; associate professor, Graceland College; Chairman, Department of Social Sciences, Graceland College.

FLETCHER, DALE T.; p. 4

825 East 2320 North, Provo, Utah 84601
B.: Logan, Utah; February 21, 1929. B.S., Utah State University, 1953; M.A., University of California, 1956; teacher, Utah public schools; teacher, BYU.

FRANCIS, RELL G.; p. 76

750 East Chase Lane, Springville, Utah 84663.
B.: Lake Shore, Utah; January 27, 1928. B.A., BYU, 1954; M.A., BYU, 1963; additional schooling, Illinois Institute of Design, University of Utah, Ohio State University, and Instituto Allende, San Miguel de Allende, Mexico; trustee, Springville High School Art Association; photo instructor, European Art Academy, 1966; best in show photography, 1962, 1966, 1967; free-lance photographer; art leader, Nebo School District, 1971. Films: documentary, *Stone Man*, featured at Mormon Festival of Arts, BYU, 1970; documentary on Mexican crafts, *¡Qué Bonita!*, for Pioneer Craft House, 1971.

GOGAN, MERRILL L.; pp. 3, 22

9454 Poppy Lane, Sandy, Utah 84070
B.: St. Johnsbury, Vermont; August 1, 1931. Art director, AD-Media, Inc.; staff artist, Florida Advertising Agency; senior illustrator, Radiator Engineering Firm, Inc., Florida; staff artist, WCSH Television; free lance, Florida and Maine; teacher, Portland School of Fine and Applied Arts; art director, *Ensign*.

GOLIGHTLY, MAX C.; See p. 53

286 East Utah Avenue, Payson, Utah
B.: Preston, Idaho; May 19, 1924. B.A., BYU; M.A., BYU; Ph.D. candidate, Southern Illinois University; secretary, NUEA, 1956-60; Utah's representative, Thespian National Drama Society, 1956-60; President, National Federation of State Poetry Society of America; winner of twenty awards in national and state poetry contests; Utah poet of the year, 1970 ("Morning of Taurus," first prize manuscript); author of many publications in drama; professor, speech and drama, BYU; director, *The Order Is Love*.

GOODLIFFE, KENT P.; p. 23

220 East 400 South, American Fork, Utah 84003
B.: Salt Lake City, Utah; June 3, 1946. BFA, BYU, 1970; graduate teaching assistant, Art Department, BYU, 1970-71; MFA candidate, BYU.

GOODMAN, HAROLD A.; p. 70

725 Stadium Avenue, Provo, Utah 84601
B.: Solomon, Arizona; July 14, 1924. B.A., University of Arizona; M.A., University of Southern California; Ed.D., University of Southern California; Chairman, Music Department, BYU; musical director and conductor, Utah Valley Symphony Orchestra, Utah Valley Youth Symphony Orchestra, Northern Arizona Orchestra, Tucson Symphony Orchestra; director of bands and orchestras, Northern Arizona State University, 1952-60; performance specialty, violin; soloist for church, school, and community recitals and concerts; membership in honorary professional societies; President, Utah Music Educators Association; member, Music Educators Research Council; Chairman, BYU Faculty Advisory Council; board member, National Association of Schools of Music.

GREEVER, MARGARET; p. 17

57 South 200 East, Provo, Utah 84601
B.: Cody, Wyoming; June 26, 1948. B.A., BYU; free-lance artist; Production Supervisor, The Naturalist Co.; Exhibit: Wyoming.

HALLIDAY, JOHN R.; *Mormon Arts, Recording I*

456 North 300 East, Provo, Utah 84601
B.: Redondo Beach, California; September 8, 1911. A.B., BYU, 1935; M.A., BYU, 1936; Ph.D., Eastman School of Music, Rochester, New York, 1939-41. Post-doctoral study: Paris, 1950; Rome, 1951; University of California at Riverside and University of Southern California, 1960-61; Madrid, 1967. Teacher, BYU, 1934-36, teacher, Eastman School of Music, 1939-41; teacher, BYU, 1941 to present; teacher, Central Washington College of Education, Ellensburg, Washington, 1957; assistant director, Salt Lake Tabernacle Choir, 1937; conductor, madrigal singers, BYU, 1951-60; conductor, concert chorus, BYU, 1936-38; conductor, oratorio choir, BYU, 1960 to present.

HANSEN, HAROLD I.; p. 58

440 East 2875 North, Provo, Utah 84601
B.: Logan, Utah; March 10, 1914. B.S., Utah State University; M.A., State University of Iowa; Ph.D., State University of Iowa; acting staff, Cleveland Play-house; co-owner and director, Grand Ledge Playhouse; director observer, Broadway production of *Gideon* with Sir Tyrone Guthrie; actor, California Tent Players; director, Hill Cumorah Pageant; director, *Tragedy of Korihor.*

HANSON, LOUISE G.; p. 58

1106 North 1750 West, Provo, Utah 84601
B.: Antelope, Oregon; June 24, 1922. B.A., BYU, 1966; M.A., BYU, 1968; teacher, BYU, 1968-70; editor, BYU Press. Published works: article, "The Feminine as Protagonist in *Hero and Leander*"; poem, "Unlawful to Litter." Dramatic works: *Korihor, Anti-Christ* and *Covenant in Gold.*

HAROLDSEN, EDWIN O.; p. 69

2827 Arapahoe Lane, Provo, Utah 84601
B.: Idaho Falls, Idaho; April 22, 1918. B.S., University of Utah, 1943; M.S., University of Utah, 1956; Ph.D., Iowa State University, 1967; regional editor, *U.S. News and World Report*; agriculture information advisor to Turkey under United States Point Four Program; feature writer, *Deseret News* and United Press International; Chairman, Communications Department, BYU.

HARRIS, JOHN B.; p. 50

356 East 1655 South, Orem, Utah 84057
B.: Los Angeles, California; July 25, 1928. B.A., BYU; M.A., BYU; Ph.D., Wayne State University; professor, English and Scandinavian, BYU.

HESLOP, J. MALAN; p. 77

80 Edgecombe Drive, Salt Lake City, Utah 84103
B.: Taylor, Utah; June 18, 1923. B.S., Utah State University, 1948; chief photographer, *Deseret News*, 1949-69; editor, *Church News.*

HUMPHREYS, EDWARD E.; p. 12

3440 20th Street, San Francisco, California 94110
B.: Portola, California; January 25, 1937. B.A., Chico State College, 1961; M.A., Chico State College, 1964; MFA, BYU, 1970; art instructor, Yuba City High School. Exhibits: one-man shows in California, Idaho, and Utah.

JOHANSEN, FRANZ; pp. 14, 66

299 East 4000 North, Provo, Utah 84601
B.: Ogden, Utah; May 10, 1928. A.B., BYU, 1955; M.A., BYU, 1956; associate professor, BYU. Winner gold first, Utah State Fair, 1959.

JOHNSON, L. ROSS; p. 13

32 South 200 East, St. George, Utah 84770
B.: Firth, Idaho; January 11, 1939. B.A., Utah State University, 1963; M.A., University of Iowa, 1965; teacher, public schools; professor of art, Dixie College.

LAYCOCK, RALPH G.; *Mormon Arts, Recording I*

508 East 600 South, Orem, Utah 84057
B.: Raymond, Alberta, Canada; February 11, 1920. M.S., Julliard School of Music; DMA, University of Southern California; member of Drake-Des Moines Symphony, Utah Symphony; director, BYU Philharmonic Orchestra, BYU Wind Symphony, Utah Valley Youth Symphony.

MARYON, EDWARD D.; p. 24

30 West 350 South, Kaysville, Utah
B.: Salt Lake City, Utah; April 5, 1931. B.A., University of Utah, 1952; MFA, University of Utah, 1956; Dean, College of Fine Arts, University of Utah. Exhibits: Utah and Idaho.

MATHEWS, CONAN E.; p. 26

460 East 400 North, Provo, Utah 84601
B.: Providence, Utah; September 16, 1907. B.S., University of Idaho; MFA, University of Utah; Chairman, Art Department, BYU; Dean, College of Fine Arts and Communications, BYU; Dean of Faculty, Boise Junior College; President, Boise Art Association. Exhibits: one-man shows in California, Idaho, and Utah.

MILLER, D. ERROL; pp. 81, 84

1738 Park Street, Salt Lake City, Utah 84105
B.: South Gate, California; July 1, 1942. B.S., BYU, 1970; BYU Student Publications, 1967-70; studied under Earl Theisen of *Look*; laboratory technician (photo) and engineering draftsman, Atomics International; photographer, Church Information Service; photographer, *Deseret News*; photographer, *Church News.*

MILLER, MARILYN R.; p. 15

1092 East 820 North, Provo, Utah 84601
B.: Paul, Idaho; May 24, 1942. B.A., BYU, 1968; MFA, BYU, 1971.

PEARSON, CAROL LYNN; pp. 13, 50

P.O. Box 843, Provo, Utah 84601
B.: Salt Lake City, Utah; September 27, 1939. B.A., BYU; M.A., BYU; teacher, Snow College. Published works: scripts, BYU Motion Picture Department; poetry, *Beginnings, The Search*; plays; magazine articles.

RINDLISBACHER, DAVID LEE; p. 5

560 South 600 West, Payson, Utah
B.: Payson, Utah; April 17, 1947. BFA, BYU; instructor, American Fork summer recreation program; instructor, adult education.

SHEPARD, CHASE; pp. 16, 18

408 North 800 East, Provo, Utah 84601
B.: Washington, D.C.; February 6, 1945. B.A., BYU, 1970; MFA, Instituto Allende (Mexico), 1972. Exhibits: gallery representation, District of Columbia, Texas, Utah.

SMITH, DENNIS; p. 68

Box 369, Alpine, Utah 84003
B.: Murray, Utah; June 16, 1942. B.A., BYU; studied at Danish Royal Academy; part-time faculty, Art Department, BYU. Exhibits: major intermountain shows; galleries, Utah, Washington, Colorado, New York, and Spain.

SMITH, GARY ERNEST; pp. 9-11, 40

Route 1, Box 414A, Provo, Utah 84601
B.: Baker, Oregon; June 29, 1942. BFA, BYU, 1970; MFA candidate, BYU; illustrator, United States Army, 1968-70; Merrill Award, 1967-70; teacher, summer workshops in Texas and New Mexico. Exhibits: one-man shows, Utah and California.

SOUTHEY, TREVOR J.; pp. 13, 31

Grove Drive, Alpine, Utah
B.: Gatooma, Rhodesia; January 12, 1940. Brighton College of Art, England, 1958-60; National Technical College (South Africa), 1960; BFA, BYU, 1967; M.A., BYU, 1969; teacher, high schools in Rhodesia and South Africa; instructor, Art Department, BYU.

TELFORD, JOHN; pp. 80-81

3976 South 1500 East, Salt Lake City, Utah
B.: Salt Lake City, Utah; December 4, 1944. Photography and graphic arts, BYU; color and black and white photography laboratory work; professional portrait and commercial photography.

THORPE, DON O.; pp. 30, 74

851 Washington Street, Salt Lake City, Utah 84101
B.: Beaver, Utah; July 31, 1934. B.S., BYU; MFA candidate, Utah State University; photo director, BYU *Banyan*, 1968; photo director, BYU *Wye Magazine*, 1968-69. Published works: photos in *Camera 35, Modern Photography*, and the *New Era.*

THORPE, EVERETT; p. 1

Utah State University, Logan, Utah
B.: Providence, Utah; August 22, 1907. B.A., Utah State University; MFA, Utah State University; professor, Utah State University. Works: portraits; murals; paintings; syndicated illustrations, LDS Bible stories; sports illustrations, *Deseret News* and *Salt Lake Tribune.*

TOBLER, TODD N.; pp. 78-79

362 North 1080 East, Provo, Utah 84601
B.: St. George, Utah; November 12, 1946. A.S., Dixie College, 1968; B.A., BYU, 1971; assistant photographer, Art Department, Dixie College; self-employed photographer.

WEAVER, MAX D.; p. 33

216 East 1864 South, Orem, Utah
B.: Layton, Utah; March 14, 1917. B.S., Utah State University, 1939; M.S., Utah State University, 1955; teacher, junior high and high schools; instructor, Utah State University; Chairman, Art Department, College of Southern Utah, 1957-61; professor, Art Department, BYU.

WHEELWRIGHT, LORIN F.; pp. v, 1, 8, 16, 19, 23, 25, 27, 32-33, 36, 40, 68, 72, 74, 82-84

2185 North 1450 East, Provo, Utah
B.: Ogden, Utah; 1909. A.B., University of Utah; M.A., University of Chicago; Ph.D., Columbia University; supervisor of music, Salt Lake City schools; organist; publisher and lithographer; composer; photographer; author; editor, the *Instructor*; editor and publisher, *The American Soroptimist*; dean, College of Fine Arts and Communications.

WHITAKER, WILLIAM; pp. 15, 19, 62, 63

Midway, Utah
B.: Chicago, Illinois; March 5, 1943. B.A., University of Utah, 1968; instructor, Art Department, BYU.

WHITMAN, CHARLES W.; p. 59

219 East 400 North, Springville, Utah 84663
B.: Montpelier, Idaho; January 28, 1933. B.A., BYU, 1957; M.A., BYU, 1958; Ph.D., University of Minnesota, 1967; teacher, Beaver High School, 1960-61; instructor, University of Minnesota, 1961-64; instructor, Chico State College, summer 1963; instructor, Sacramento State College, 1964-65; assistant professor in dramatic arts, BYU, since 1965. Stage credits: Hill Cumorah Pageant, Cleveland Play House, Oregon Shakespeare Festival, Dallas Theatre Center, Minnesota Centennial Showboat Company, Punchinello Players, Ledges Playhouse.

WOODBURY, LAEL J.; pp. 53-60, 64, 75, 76

1303 Locust Lane, Provo, Utah 84601
B.: Fairview, Idaho; July 3, 1927. B.S., Utah State University; M.A., BYU; Ph.D., University of Illinois; Chairman, Department of Speech and Dramatic Arts, BYU; director, experimental theater, Bowling Green State University; director of acting and directing, University of Iowa; guest professor, Colorado State College; producer and director, Ledges Playhouse; director of centennial pageants at Nephi, Utah, and Las Vegas, Nevada; Karl G. Maeser Creative Arts Award, BYU, 1971; president, Rocky Mountain Theatre Conference; associate dean, College of Fine Arts and Communications, BYU.

YOUNG, JAMES L.; p. 20

732 North 500 East, Price, Utah 84501
B.: Price, Utah; November 29, 1937. A.S., College of Eastern Utah; B.S., BYU; M.A., BYU; MFA, Utah State University; graduate assistant, Education Department, BYU; teacher, Corvallis High School, Corvallis, Oregon; member, Carbon County School District Board of Education; teacher, College of Eastern Utah; Chairman, Art Department, College of Eastern Utah. Exhibits: Utah and surrounding states.

PICTURE IDENTIFICATION OF PERFORMERS

(Left to Right, Top to Bottom)

W-2 FORM, p. 41: Janice Jenkins, Joyce Jenson, Richard B. West, Paul M. Searle, Jane Luke

THE ORDER IS LOVE, p. 52: Rob Nuismer, Diana Lynne Harris; p. 54: Curt Mortensen, Paul Miller, Lee Andra Marsh, Jane Luke, Douglas Volt, Robert Pomo, Blaine Jensen, Robert Stoddard; p. 55: Jim Gadd, Arlen Card, Mark Van Bloom, Paul Miller, Matthew Mills, Blaine Chambers, Paul Corrington, Mark Trunnell; (below) Rain Conger, Sue Plumb, Del Mandarino

W-2 FORM, p. 56: Richard B. West, Joyce Jenson, Janice Jenkins, Blaine Chambers

THE TRAGEDY OF KORIHOR, p. 58: William Hazlett, Janet Swenson, Candace Woolley, Mark Stabler

THE APOSTATE, p. 59: Mark Hopkin, Barta Lee Heiner, Dean A. Davis, David Cowley, John Huntington, Joseph Psuik, III

MORMON VIGNETTE, p. 60: Kathy Merrill (with guitar), Barbara Clark, Greg Reeder, Jill Carter, Charles Burrell, Donna James, Lon Bowen, Sam Crain, Steven White

MORMON VIGNETTE, p. 61: Jill Carter, Sam Crain

MUSICIANS, p. 70: *Harp*, Janice Clark Bills; *French Horns*, Stephen Taylor, Mark Bassett, Barbara Reeder, Vincent Echols; *Flutes*, Peggy Howell, Charlotte Brown Day, Roger Watson; *Vocalists*, Sandra Taylor, Kirsten Hemp, Lois Johnson, Jane Ann Dalbini, Constance Smith, Starla Swenson; p. 71: *Cello*, Phyllis Baker Milner; *Violin*, Patrice Anderson

DANCERS, p. 73: Paul Corrington, Connie Burton

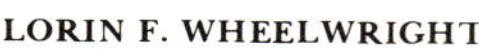

A PRAYER

O Divine Artist, God of us all,

Who fashioned man and placed within his bosom
A Spirit, like unto Thine:

Grant unto us, Thy humble servants,

. . . the *patience* Thou hast shown in
sculpturing this earth,
. . . the *genius* of Thy hand in painting
rainbows in the flowers,
. . . the *tenderness* of Thy love which fills
the heavens with song,
. . . the *perception* of Thine eyes which illumines
the night with stars, and
. . . the *generosity* of Thy Spirit which gives to us
Thy Beloved Son.

Lift our souls!
Inspire us to help others that they may see

Thy good works, and
Become as Thou art —
A creator of beauty in the hearts of men.

— In Jesus' name,

AMEN

LORIN F. WHEELWRIGHT

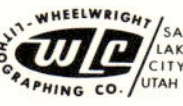